Fix the Experience, Keep the Customer

10 THINGS THEY HATE ABOUT YOU

A CX Playbook For Leaders

LANCE GRUNER

Library of Congress Control Number: 2025918267

Paperback ISBN: 978-1-969063-03-9
Hardcover ISBN: 978-1-969063-04-6

1. Main category—Nonfiction › Business & Investing › Marketing & Sales › Customer Relations
2. Other category—Nonfiction › Business & Investing › Management & Leadership › Total Quality Management
3. Other category—Nonfiction › Business & Investing › Management & Leadership › Management › Strategic Management

AR
PRESS

Published by: American Real Publishing
americanrealpublishing.com

This book is dedicated to my mom, whose support and encouragement through the years made me reach for the stars and pursue my dreams.

TABLE OF CONTENTS

FOREWORD

There are business books that are thought-provoking. There are business books that are practical. And then there are business books that change the way you see your customers forever.

This is one of those books.

I've had the privilege of knowing Lance for years, and if there's one thing I can tell you, it's this: He understands customers in a way most leaders never will. Not because he's read the latest industry reports or tracked the hottest customer trends, but because he's spent years living in the reality of what makes customers stay—and what makes them walk away forever.

Most companies don't lose customers because of one bad interaction. They lose them because of a series of small, frustrating moments that build up over time. And the worst part? They don't even see it happening. The call that never gets returned. The support agent who doesn't have the right answer. The refund that takes two weeks to process. The app that crashes at the worst possible moment. The cancellation process that feels like an escape room with no exit.

It's these everyday failures that drive customers away, not competitors.

And yet, most leaders continue to track the wrong things—survey scores, quarterly retention rates, and "success metrics" that look great in reports but fail to capture the real, human experience of the customer.

That's why this book is so powerful. It doesn't just diagnose why customers leave but forces you to feel what they feel, walk in their frustration, and finally see the problems that have been hiding in plain sight.

It's also a book that makes you uncomfortable because once you see these problems, you can't unsee them. Once you recognize that your company is making mistakes that drive customers away, you can't go back to business as usual.

And that's exactly what makes Lance Gruner such a rare voice in the world of customer experience. He doesn't just talk about customer pain points. He fights for them. He doesn't just present data. He tells the stories behind the numbers.

He doesn't just push for better CX strategy. He pushes for companies to rethink everything from their policies and processes to their very definition of success.

If you're a CEO, a CX leader, a frontline manager, or anyone who touches the customer experience in any way, this book will challenge you to look beyond your current metrics, step into the shoes of your customers, and fix the things that are quietly driving them away.

The brands that survive and thrive in the next decade won't be the ones with the biggest advertising budgets or the most aggressive sales strategies. They will be the ones that truly listen, truly care, and truly build companies customers want to stay with.

This book will show you how to become one of those companies.

Now, turn the page and prepare to see your business—and your customers—differently than you ever have before.

Shep Hyken
Chief Amazement Officer, Shepard Productions
Author of: *I'll Be Back*, *Be Amazing or Go Home*, and *The Convenience Revolution*

INTRODUCTION

Fix the Experience, Keep the Customer!

Customers are leaving, and it's not random. It rarely starts with a bang.

A once-loyal customer cancels their subscription. A long-time client stops responding to outreach. A repeat buyer vanishes without a trace. At first, it looks like routine churn. But patterns emerge. They didn't just leave. They left frustrated after waiting on hold too long, after being transferred too many times, after being charged for something they didn't agree to. And they didn't go quietly. They wrote reviews. They told their friends. They made sure others didn't make the same mistake.

This is how companies lose customers today—not through massive, catastrophic breakdowns but through thousands of small failures that pile up until the customer decides they've had enough. Most companies don't realize they are the problem until it's too late. The question is:

Are you one of them?

THE UNCOMFORTABLE TRUTH

It's easy to blame pricing or market dynamics, but more often than not the reason customers walk away is much more personal and much more preventable. They leave because they feel invisible. Because the experience is too hard. Because no one seems to care. Over the course of my career in leading global operations and customer care for some of the world's most recognizable brands, I've had a front-row seat to why customers stay and why they leave. The patterns are painfully clear. Customers aren't leaving over price or product. They're leaving because the experience pushes them out the door. And what drives them away? Ten recurring failures that have nothing to do with strategy slides and everything to do with how companies operate every single day.

Your teams aren't trained. Your policies are built to protect the business, not the customer. Your billing is confusing. Your platforms fail at the worst possible time. Your silence after a mistake feels like indifference. You overpromise, underdeliver, and then act surprised when customers don't return.

These failures don't just frustrate customers, they erode trust, cost you loyalty, and cost you growth.

I wrote this book because too many leaders still believe customer experience is someone else's job, that it's a "service issue," that it doesn't impact real business outcomes. They're wrong. Customer experience is a *leadership* issue. It's a *financial* issue. It's a *growth strategy*. And when done right, it's a competitive *advantage* no pricing promotion or brand campaign can match.

This is not another abstract business book filled with empty frameworks and consulting jargon. It's a playbook designed for leaders who are ready to get real about why customers are leaving and how to fix it.

- Part One exposes the ten things customers hate most. Each chapter explores one of these failures, backed by real-world case studies, operational breakdowns, and the business cost of inaction.
- Part Two is about the fix. You'll learn how to measure what matters, how to challenge internal resistance, how to be the customer's voice when no one else will, and how to lead CX from the inside out.

This book is for anyone who shapes the customer experience—directly or indirectly—including:

- Executives who are setting strategic priorities.
- Marketing and product leaders designing the customer journey.
- Digital, data, and operations teams delivering the day-to-day experience.
- The frontline teams—the unsung heroes of most organizations who live in the gap between customer expectation and company execution.

The customer experience is not one team's job. It's everyone's job. And when it's broken, it's everyone's problem.

You didn't pick up this book by accident. You already know there's something not working. Maybe your scores are slipping. Maybe your teams are burning out. Maybe you just know the customer is frustrated and can't figure out why. So the question isn't whether experience is broken but what you're going to do about it. Are you going to keep tracking the same KPIs and hoping things improve? Or are you ready to lead the kind of transformation that actually keeps customers? Because the best companies don't just talk about experience. They live it. They *walk the property*. They fix the small things before they become big ones and they build a culture where the customer doesn't need to yell to be heard. This book will show you how.

Let's get to work.

Lance

PART ONE

The Problem

CHAPTER 1

The Competence Crisis

Lack of knowledgeable and trained people is not just a problem—it's the single biggest frustration customers say they experience. It's the moment when expectations collapse into disappointment and trust begins to erode. "Why does no one know how to help me?" This question echoes in the mind of every frustrated customer who has ever felt abandoned in the midst of a service crisis. It is the question that underpins a profound failure—a failure not of technology, products, or even strategy but of knowledge and empowerment. In today's hypercompetitive marketplace where every second of a customer's time is invaluable, a single moment of ignorance can shatter trust and drive customers away forever.

I once sat in on a customer service call at a global travel company—a brand that marketed itself as the gold standard for high-end, stress-free vacations. The customer on the line was polite, patient, and clearly frustrated. A glitch in the booking system had canceled their honeymoon reservation. What should've been a simple recovery—one click, one rebooking, one sincere apology—turned into a forty-five-minute ordeal that ended with a vague promise to "escalate this to another team."

Why? Because the representative had no idea how the system worked. No empowerment. No training. Just a script.

I remember watching the rep flip between windows, frantically searching the knowledge base, mumbling canned lines like "I completely understand your frustration," while escalating a ticket into the void. She wasn't lazy. She wasn't rude. She was unprepared and set up to fail by a system that didn't invest in her ability to succeed.

This isn't an isolated incident. Across industries and sectors, countless businesses face a silent epidemic that drains revenue and erodes brand loyalty. The hidden cost of ignorance is not merely the inconvenience of waiting on hold; it is the cumulative loss of customer confidence, loyalty, and ultimately, revenue. In a world where speed and competence are prized above all, every minute wasted on inefficient support is a lost opportunity to build trust and a lasting relationship.

For many companies, the root cause of this crisis lies not in a lack of technological tools but in a failure to invest in the one asset that truly makes a difference: knowledgeable, empowered employees. When frontline representatives are ill-prepared to address even the most basic queries, the entire customer experience is compromised. It is not enough to have cutting-edge AI, robust self-service portals, or an extensive CRM system if the people behind these tools are left to flounder in a sea of outdated information and rigid protocols.

Today's customer service landscape is littered with "good enough" service: polite greetings, escalation protocols, and resolution windows that stretch into days or weeks. What's missing? Competence. Confidence. Ownership. And the irony is, most companies don't lose customers because of one big blow-up. They lose them in tiny moments of breakdown. Missed expectations. Delayed resolutions. Halfhearted apologies. A dozen small failures that compound into churn.

WHEN YOUR PEOPLE AREN'T TRAINED, YOUR BRAND ISN'T READY.

Consider the reality: A McKinsey study reveals that 78 percent of customers rank speaking with a knowledgeable representative as the single most important element of a great service experience. Yet, an astonishing 63 percent of customers, according to Forrester, often feel they know more about the product or issue than the rep assisting them. This discrepancy is not just a minor operational hiccup—it is a systemic failure that underpins a massive loss of trust. When customers are forced to confront employees who lack the requisite knowledge, they begin to doubt whether the company can ever truly address their needs.

The financial repercussions of this disconnect are staggering. A study by Accenture estimates that US businesses lose a combined total of $1.6 trillion each year as customers abandon brands in search of more competent service. These losses are not predominantly due to inferior pricing, subpar product quality, or aggressive competition; rather, they stem from the intangible, yet critical, belief that "someone will help me." And when that belief is shattered by every interaction, even the most loyal customers will eventually walk away.

And in today's experience economy, service missteps don't just disappear quietly. They travel. A single poor interaction becomes a screenshot, a social media post, a scathing review. The impact compounds, and brand reputations—years in the making—can be undone in a day. Not because your marketing missed the mark, but because someone on the front line couldn't deliver when it counted.

Frontline competence isn't a soft skill. It's a brand promise. Delivered—or broken—every single day.

THE HIGH COST OF INCOMPETENCE

LET'S TALK ABOUT THE BOTTOM LINE.

According to a 2023 PwC study, 32 percent of customers will walk away from a brand they love after just one bad experience. One. Not a pattern. Not a scandal. A single incident. That's the margin for error companies are working with now. And what's one of the fastest ways to create a bad experience? Incompetence.

The 2024 Microsoft Global Customer Experience Report found that 72 percent of consumers expect agents to already know who they are and what they've interacted with previously. But 65 percent of service reps say they struggle to access even basic customer data in real time. That disconnect is more than a technical glitch. It's a trust killer.

A 2023 Salesforce survey revealed that 68 percent of customers feel like most companies treat them as a number, not a person. That's not a complaint about tone. It's a reaction to being on the phone with someone who clearly doesn't understand the product, the problem, or how to help.

In the hospitality industry alone, McKinsey reports that poorly handled service interactions can reduce repeat bookings by up to 40 percent. In banking and insurance, the consequences are even more severe, often triggering regulatory complaints, legal exposure, and reputational damage that can take years to recover from.

And this isn't just about customer fallout. Let's talk about the internal cost.

Every unresolved interaction becomes a multitouch escalation. Every escalation requires senior intervention. And every hour spent fixing preventable problems is an hour not spent adding value. Meanwhile, the frontline employees who do know what they're doing burn out. They become the unofficial QA department—fielding handoffs, correcting errors, and carrying the emotional load of a broken system.

Here's the ripple effect:

- An untrained employee creates delays.
- Delays lead to escalations.
- Escalations create internal cost.
- Internal cost erodes margin.
- Meanwhile, the customer leaves—and tells ten friends why.

That's how companies lose millions. Not in the boardroom. Not in a major crisis. But quietly, invisibly, through everyday incompetence that goes unaddressed for years.

THE ANATOMY OF A CRISIS

At the heart of this crisis is a chain reaction of missteps and systemic over-sights. In many organizations, training is viewed as an optional cost rather than a vital investment. During budget cuts or financial downturns, training programs are often the first to be slashed. This short-sighted approach creates an environment where employees are thrust into their roles with insufficient knowledge and support. As a result, every customer interaction becomes a potential disaster, as underprepared representatives struggle to provide solutions.

Moreover, the high turnover rate in customer service positions only compounds the problem. With turnover rates hovering between 30 and 45 percent annually, companies find themselves in a perpetual cycle of recruiting, onboarding, and retraining new hires—many of whom leave before they can fully grasp the nuances of their roles. This constant churn not only drains resources but also means that even the most well-designed training programs are rendered ineffective if employees do not stick around long enough to apply what they've learned.

Even when training initiatives are in place, they are frequently fragmented and disjointed. Information is scattered across outdated manuals, siloed knowledge bases, and disconnected platforms. In one revealing study by McKinsey, employees were found to spend an average of 1.8 hours per day simply searching for the information they need to assist customers. That adds up to nearly a full workday each week lost to inefficiency—a loss that directly translates into a diminished capacity to serve customers effectively.

Yet perhaps the most critical flaw in many customer service models is the lack of empowerment. In many organizations, representatives are not given the authority to resolve issues on the spot. Instead, they are forced to escalate even minor problems to higher-ups, creating delays and further frustrating customers. This rigid, bureaucratic structure communicates a clear message: Decisions matter more to the process than to the customer. And when customers sense that their concerns are being passed around rather than directly addressed, their trust in the brand erodes quickly.

WHY THIS PROBLEM PERSISTS

SO WHY, IN 2025, IS THIS STILL HAPPENING?

Because training is expensive. Because enablement is hard. And because too many companies still see it as a cost center instead of what it really is—a strategic asset.

In most boardrooms, customer service isn't top of mind unless something's on fire. Budgets go first to growth, then to marketing, then to tech. And by the time someone raises their hand to advocate for frontline development, the pie has already been sliced.

There's a reason training budgets are often the first to be cut and the last to be reinstated. The ROI isn't immediate. And in a quarterly culture, long-term value doesn't always win.

But the problem isn't just money. It's mindset.

Add to that:

- High turnover in customer-facing roles
- Outsourced operations with inconsistent standards
- Overreliance on scripts and automation
- A leadership culture that prioritizes speed and scale over clarity and care

And most damaging of all: The false belief that a friendly tone and a good toolset can replace real expertise.

Training has been conflated with onboarding. Enablement has been reduced to compliance. And roles that are most visible to the customer have become the least invested in internally. That's not a cost-saving strategy. That's a churn accelerator.

I've worked with global organizations across travel, fintech, hospitality, and SaaS. The pattern is consistent. As companies scale, they invest in product, pricing, and promotion. But they cut corners where customers feel it the most—at the front line. The result? A brand that sounds great in the investor deck but falls apart in a real-life moment of need.

Ironically, it's these "low-skill" roles that make or break customer loyalty. The customer doesn't see your strategic roadmap. They see your agent. They hear the hold music. They experience the transfer. That moment is the brand.

When the person on the line doesn't have the tools, the training, or the trust to solve the problem—they don't just fail the customer. They fail the promise your brand made.

It's not sustainable. And it's definitely not a strategy.

WHAT CUSTOMERS REALLY WANT

It's easy to believe that customers today are unreasonable or impossible to please. But the truth is far simpler—and far more fixable. What customers really want is clarity. Confidence. And the feeling that they're in capable, competent hands.

They want to be treated like human beings, not case numbers. They want to speak to someone who can actually help—not just someone who sounds friendly while transferring them into oblivion.

According to Salesforce's 2024 State of the Connected Customer report:

- 84 percent of customers say being treated like a person—not a ticket—is what makes them loyal.
- 79 percent expect consistent experiences across departments.
- 71 percent say they'll switch brands after multiple poor service experiences.

But here's the kicker: 92 percent of customers say they would stay loyal to a brand that solved their issue quickly and effectively—even if the original problem was frustrating.

That's the blueprint right there. Customers don't expect perfection. But they do expect progress. They expect the person they talk to knows the product. Knows the system. Knows the policy. And when they don't? They expect someone to take ownership—and fix it.

Because at the end of the day, competence is what communicates care. It says, "You matter enough for us to be ready for you." It builds trust. It earns forgiveness. And it turns a problem into a moment of loyalty.

In a 2023 study by Qualtrics XM Institute, customers were five times more likely to recommend a company that "resolves issues quickly and effectively" than one with a great marketing campaign. Why? Because resolution builds credibility. Not marketing.

Customers don't want over polished scripts. They don't want empathy theater. They want someone who listens, understands, and knows what to do next.

Competence might not be flashy, but in a world full of chatbots and call transfers, it's the most powerful differentiator you've got.

TRAINING VS. ENABLEMENT

Too many companies still think of training as a checkbox. A one-time event. A couple of PowerPoint slides. Maybe a buddy shadow session on Day One, and then it's off to the races.

That's not training. That's orientation.

What today's frontline teams actually need is enablement—an ongoing system of support, learning, and reinforcement that helps them stay confident, current, and capable.

Here's the difference:

- Training is how you get someone started.
- Enablement is how you keep them successful.
- Coaching is how you make them better.

Enablement isn't just about product knowledge. It's about decision-making. Empathy. Conflict resolution. Policy navigation. It's about equipping people not just to do the job—but to do it well, under pressure, in real time.

Companies that get this right don't measure training completion—they measure readiness. They use real customer scenarios. They test judgment, not memorization. They simulate tension, not ideal outcomes. And they evolve content alongside the business, so no one is left behind.

Enablement also requires organizational alignment. If marketing changes the customer promise, service needs to be prepared. If product launches a new feature, frontline teams need to be fluent before customers are. If legal tightens the refund policy, everyone needs to understand how to explain it—not just enforce it.

Best-in-class organizations like American Express, Zappos, and Atlassian have embraced enablement as a core part of their CX strategy. Amex, for example, measures agent effectiveness based not on call time but on "first-call ownership." Zappos built an internal library of service scenarios with agent-led best practices, constantly updated based on feedback loops. These aren't perks. They're operating principles.

In companies where service is seen as strategic, enablement is embedded. It's continuous. It's visible. And it's respected.

Because nothing slows down a high-performing team like low-confidence people making high-stakes decisions without support.

SCRIPT FATIGUE AND ROBOTIC INTERACTIONS

Let's be honest customers aren't asking for Shakespeare. But they are asking for sincerity.

And they can spot scripted responses a mile away.

We've trained an entire generation of agents to be compliant—but not confident. They read from carefully worded statements designed to sound helpful but rarely are. And the result? A support experience that feels robotic, disconnected, and maddeningly ineffective.

Here's what customers hear:

"I'm sorry for the inconvenience you're experiencing."

"I understand how frustrating that must be."

"Let me look into that for you."

There's nothing wrong with these phrases—on their own. But when delivered without presence, without authority, and without variation, they ring hollow.

A 2023 Gartner study found that 63 percent of customers felt more frustrated after speaking to a live agent than they did when using self-service—largely because of scripted, nonempowering responses.

Scripts should be guidelines—not gospel. They should give employees a foundation, not a cage. When someone's reading to you like they're performing for a compliance scorecard, trust erodes. And so does patience.

The solution? Train for judgment. Create space for improvisation. Role-play difficult conversations. Teach tone. Teach timing. Teach how to speak in the brand's voice without losing your own.

Great service is like jazz. It's structured, but it's also alive. And the companies that understand this give their people the tools and trust to deliver human service—not just scripted transactions.

Southwest Airlines, for instance, encourages employees to bring their personalities into the conversation. It's not about being funny or quirky—it's about being real. That authenticity builds connection—and connection builds loyalty.

Customers want to feel like they're having a conversation, not checking off boxes. And the brands that win are the ones who empower their teams to sound, think, and care like real people.

FRONTLINE OWNERSHIP AND EMPOWERMENT

If I could offer one piece of advice to every executive responsible for customer experience, it would be this:

Give your people the power to say yes.

Yes to refunds when they make sense.

Yes to rerouting a package.

Yes to solving a problem without needing five levels of approval.

Ownership at the front line is the fastest way to resolve issues and build loyalty. It replaces hesitation with momentum. It transforms frustration into relief. And most importantly, it builds trust—both inside and outside the company.

Consider the Ritz-Carlton's now-famous $2,000 rule. Any employee can spend up to $2,000 to resolve a guest issue without asking for permission. Do they use it often? No. But that's not the point. The authority speaks volumes. It tells the employee, "We trust you." And it tells the customer, "We care."

I worked with a large telecom brand that rolled out a frontline resolution pilot in its billing department. Instead of requiring agents to escalate disputes over $25, they gave them authority to credit up to $150 if it was the right thing to do. Complaints dropped. First-call resolution rose. Refund volume barely changed. And most tellingly? Employee satisfaction skyrocketed.

Research from Harvard Business Review shows that companies with high levels of employee empowerment see a 50 percent greater likelihood of customer satisfaction scores exceeding expectations. Why? Because people are proud of the work they're trusted to own.

Empowered teams don't just handle service—they deliver it. They see themselves as problem-solvers, not rule-enforcers. And when you build systems that support ownership, the results show up in every corner of the business: faster resolution, higher CSAT, lower attrition, stronger brand equity.

Want to elevate your brand in the eyes of the customer? Start by elevating the decisions you let your employees make.

THE ROLE OF LEADERSHIP

Let's be clear: Leadership owns the experience. If your frontline teams are untrained, unsupported, or uninspired, that's not an HR issue—it's a leadership failure.

Executives don't have to sit through every training session or jump on every call, but they do have to show up in meaningful, visible ways. When leaders prioritize service readiness—when they talk about it, measure it, invest in it—it signals to the rest of the organization that competence is strategic, not optional.

Culture cascades. When executives model learning, responsiveness, and care, the rest of the company follows. When they ignore it, the organization learns to do the same.

The best-run companies make customer experience a leadership conversation—not just a departmental one. They don't limit their dashboards to NPS or CSAT. They dig deeper: agent readiness, time-to-proficiency, coaching frequency, knowledge base usage, escalation ratios. These are the real indicators of whether your front line can deliver on your brand promise.

One hospitality company's COO I worked with started every quarterly business review with a fifteen-minute "voice of the customer" session. Real calls. Real transcripts. Real feedback—good, bad, and uncomfortable. It wasn't a gimmick. It was a grounding moment. It made the customer real and reminded every executive in the room why their work mattered.

Another enterprise B2B platform added CX deep dives to their board materials. Not just metrics, but stories. Escalations that went wrong. Successes that were hard-won. The board didn't just ask about growth. They asked about customer trust.

You can't drive frontline excellence from a spreadsheet. You lead it by walking the floor. By asking, "What's in your way?" By removing friction. By listening more than you report.

Leadership isn't just about setting the vision—it's about clearing the path. And when competence is your goal, that means making it a top-down, full-company imperative.

TOOLS, TECH, AND CONTINUOUS LEARNING

We are surrounded by technology that can make learning easier, faster, and more effective than ever before. So why are so many customer service teams still operating like it's 2010?

The issue isn't access to tools—it's how we use them.

Too many companies treat their LMS like a digital filing cabinet. Static PDFs. One-size-fits-all videos. Annual compliance modules. That's not enablement. That's content archiving.

Modern platforms like Lessonly, 360Learning, and SAP Litmos offer interactive, role-based learning experiences. They allow teams to train in the flow of work, measure comprehension in real time, and update content as the business evolves. These aren't just tools—they're engines for agility.

AI-powered platforms are taking it even further. Observe.AI and Balto analyze live calls to coach in real time. They highlight tone, empathy, silence, keyword use—flagging where help is needed while the call is happening. This isn't the future. It's the present.

High-performing organizations use this tech not just to monitor—but to improve. They embed learning into daily rhythms: morning huddles, shift recaps, weekly sprints. They use peer-led sessions, rotating facilitators, and bite-sized modules built from real tickets.

At Airbnb, CX teams host weekly "Case Clinics" where agents walk through tough service moments, share learnings, and build new scenarios for training. It's collaborative. It's relevant. And it creates a living curriculum fueled by the customer voice.

Enablement shouldn't be siloed. Learning must flow between functions—product to support, marketing to service, engineering to ops. The best teams don't just teach—they cocreate.

Continuous learning isn't about pushing more content. It's about ensuring your people are always prepared for what's next. And with customers evolving faster than ever, what's next is always just around the corner.

WHAT GREAT LOOKS LIKE

Exceptional customer experiences don't happen by accident. They are the result of intentional design, empowered teams, and a company-wide commitment to competence. If you want to understand the difference between companies that deliver exceptional service and those that simply get by, look at how they invest in their people.

Take Ritz-Carlton. Every employee—regardless of role—receives intensive training when they're hired, and ongoing development throughout their career. But it's not just the amount of training that matters—it's the intent. They train for empowerment. Employees are given the autonomy to resolve guest issues on the spot, up to $2,000 per guest, per incident, without having to ask for permission. That's not about cost. That's about trust.

And it shows. The brand is known not just for delivering luxury, but for delivering consistency, recovery, and care. Even when things go wrong, customers walk away impressed.

Chewy is another great example. Their customer service reps are empowered to act quickly, send handwritten cards, offer thoughtful gestures when a pet passes away, or provide proactive support based on prior orders. These employees aren't just reading a script—they're acting like brand ambassadors who care. The result? A fiercely loyal customer base and industry-wide admiration.

Delta Air Lines took a bold approach post-COVID by reinvesting in its service model. They retrained frontline agents in emotional intelligence, gave them more authority in high-friction moments, and restructured incentives to reward service recovery—not just issue avoidance. The result? They climbed industry satisfaction rankings and gained loyalty from passengers who appreciated the human touch in a digital-first world.

And consider Shopify. Their support team isn't just trained in technical troubleshooting. They're trained in empathy for small business owners. Agents are expected to understand the customer's context—not just the function of the button that broke. That shift—from transactional support to strategic partnership—has made Shopify not just a platform, but a trusted business ally.

What do these companies share?

- A commitment to treating training as a strategic asset, not a checkbox.
- A belief that frontline teams are stewards of the brand.
- Clear authority structures that favor action over bureaucracy.
- Ongoing investments in coaching, recognition, and internal storytelling that celebrate moments of customer care.

These aren't perks. They're the pillars of cultures that prioritize competence.

Even in industries where technology dominates—like fintech, health tech, and SaaS—the companies that consistently outperform are those that treat service as a differentiator, not an afterthought.

Competence doesn't just keep customers satisfied. It earns trust. It drives retention. And it elevates the brand—one interaction at a time.

THE FIX: A ROADMAP TO COMPETENCE

A competence crisis doesn't resolve itself. It requires deliberate strategy, leadership alignment, and organizational commitment. To elevate frontline performance, companies must go beyond sporadic training programs and adopt a system of enablement that is continuous, measurable, and integrated into how the business operates.

Here's a practical roadmap to build and sustain competence at scale:

- Audit reality, not assumptions.

  Start with truth. Sit in on calls. Watch chat logs. Walk the floor. What do your customers really experience? What do your agents really struggle with? Too many leaders operate with outdated assumptions. The best ones get curious and get close.

- Reframe training as continuous enablement.

  Training can't be a one-time event. Build learning into the flow of work. Use real-world scenarios. Create learning paths that evolve with the employee. Update your knowledge base weekly—not quarterly. Celebrate learning, not just compliance.

- Teach judgment, not just policy.

  Anyone can read a policy. Competent agents know how to interpret it. Use scenario training to build nuance. Teach people to manage ambiguity, resolve tension, and handle emotional conversations. Policy gets you legal. Judgment gets you loyalty.

- Empower first, escalate second.

  Redesign workflows to encourage frontline decision-making. Create clear guardrails but trust people within them. Track outcomes and coach with context. Empowerment isn't chaos—it's controlled autonomy, supported by coaching.

- Invest in coaches, not just supervisors.

  Too many managers are glorified administrators. Rebuild their roles as performance multipliers. Give them time, tools, and training to coach—not just track metrics. Measure them on growth, not just throughput.

- Use tech to support, not replace.

  Invest in AI that makes your people smarter. Use knowledge systems that are intelligent and intuitive. Leverage call intelligence to surface coaching moments. But remember: Tech supports great service—it doesn't deliver it alone.

- Recognize and reward competence.

What gets recognized gets repeated. Create internal recognition programs that highlight exceptional service. Reward moments of smart judgment, fast recovery, and customer delight—not just speed.

- Make competence a C-suite metric.

  Put it on the scorecard. Include customer trust signals in board reviews. Correlate enablement investments with performance metrics like retention, CLTV, and resolution speed. What you measure at the top becomes a mandate at every level.

This is not just an ops initiative. It's a business strategy.

Competence is the new battleground. And the organizations that embrace it—not as a training problem, but as a cultural advantage—will lead.

Because when your people show up capable, confident, and ready, your brand doesn't just look better. It performs better.

WHY IT MATTERS NOW MORE THAN EVER

What customers remember isn't how shiny your app was or how catchy your slogan sounded. They remember how you made them feel—especially when things went wrong.

The moments that define loyalty aren't always flawless transactions. They're recovery moments. They're moments of tension turned into trust. And more often than not, they hinge on whether your team was equipped, empowered, and confident enough to do the right thing.

We've entered a new era where competence isn't just a service benchmark—it's a brand differentiator. In a world where customer expectations are higher than ever and attention spans are shorter than ever, companies don't get three chances anymore. They get one.

That single moment—when a customer needs help, hits a wall, or runs into friction—is where your brand promise is tested. And in that moment, your team is either ready or they're not.

Trust is no longer built in campaigns. It's built in interactions. And that trust can be reinforced—or eroded—by the least senior person on your payroll.

In a 2023 PwC global survey, 73 percent of customers said customer experience helps drive their buying decision, and 60 percent said they'd stop doing business with a brand after just one poor interaction—even if they loved the product. Let that sink in: Even if your product is excellent, your customer experience can still lose the customer.

This is not the work of one department. It's the mandate of an entire organization.

Executives must set the tone. People leaders must reinforce the standard. Technology must enable—not replace—human judgment. And everyone, from the boardroom to the front line, must understand that competence isn't a soft skill. It's a business imperative.

If your people can't own the interaction, resolve the issue, or confidently guide the customer—you don't have a service problem. You have a trust problem.

Competence is not a cost. It's not a checkbox. It's a promise you make every time a customer reaches out. And it's either kept—or broken—at the very edge of your business.

Because people remember how you made them feel—and they remember who got it right when it mattered.

Your brand is only as strong as the least prepared person representing it. So, make sure they're not just ready—make sure they're exceptional.

Key Takeaways

1. Customers Don't Want to Be Known—They Want to Be Noticed

Customers aren't asking for flattery. They want relevance, recognition, and responsiveness. When companies treat interactions as transactions, they miss the opportunity to create loyalty by making people feel seen.

2. Frontline Feedback Is a Leading Indicator—and You're Ignoring It

Your agents, chats, and survey comments are telling you exactly what's broken. If you're not listening to the patterns or giving weight to the emotional tone behind them, you're choosing ignorance over insight.

3. Empathy Isn't Just Soft Skill—It's Operational Data

Recognizing the customer's context isn't kindness; it's competitive advantage. Companies that embed empathy into product design, service flows, and feedback loops outperform those that treat it as "extra."

CHAPTER 2

Long Wait Times & No Respect for My Time

The silent killer of customer loyalty started with a hold tone. A customer—loyal for years, always paid on time, referred others—called to resolve a small billing error. She waited. Ten minutes became twenty. After thirty-five minutes on hold, she got through. The rep was pleasant but powerless. He transferred her to someone else. Another ten-minute hold. The new rep couldn't locate the history. She had to explain everything again.

The issue? A twelve-dollar charge. The result? A canceled account and a scathing LinkedIn post seen by over forty thousand people.

This isn't an outlier. It's the new normal. And it's killing customer loyalty quietly but efficiently—one wasted minute at a time.

We've all been there: waiting in a never-ending phone queue, dealing with a chatbot that can't understand basic queries, refreshing an app that keeps glitching. These experiences don't just test patience—they chip away at brand trust.

For the customer, the message is clear: Your time doesn't matter. And that message, repeated in microfrictions and delays, eventually becomes intolerable.

No loyalty program, no promotional email, no NPS survey follow-up can undo the message sent when a company wastes someone's time.

WHY TIME IS THE NEW CURRENCY

In today's experience economy, time isn't just a resource. It's a decision driver. Customers are no longer comparing your service to your closest competitor. They're comparing you to Uber, Amazon, DoorDash, and Apple.

Why? Because those companies have set a new baseline. One-click checkout. Delivery in hours. No-hassle returns. Real-time updates. These aren't luxuries anymore—they're expectations.

According to PwC, 52 percent of consumers would pay more for greater speed and efficiency. Salesforce found that 83 percent of customers expect immediate interaction when they contact a company. Not fast. Immediate.

Think about that. If your definition of "responsive" is a twenty-four-hour email reply window, you're already behind.

Time is emotional. It's not just about seconds and minutes—it's about respect. It's about trust. When you save someone time, they feel valued. When you waste it, they feel dismissed.

And here's the twist: Companies waste customer time even when they think they're doing the right thing. That two-minute survey after every interaction? That chatbot that takes five steps to transfer to a human? That "your call is very important to us" hold message on a loop for twenty-seven minutes?

Every one of those moments sends a message. And the message is: "We value our systems more than your schedule."

In a landscape where customer choice is vast and loyalty is thin, how you manage time is how customers measure you.

THE HIDDEN COSTS OF MAKING CUSTOMERS WAIT

MOST COMPANIES DON'T REALIZE HOW EXPENSIVE WASTED TIME REALLY IS.

We track conversion. We track churn. We track cost to serve. But rarely do we put a number on the minutes we ask customers to spend in limbo.

But the cost is real. And it's growing.

Every minute a customer spends stuck in a queue, repeating themselves, waiting for follow-up, or clicking through unclear portals adds invisible costs to your business:

- Operational drag—Longer interactions create backlog, increase staffing needs, and reduce agility.
- Brand erosion—Customers don't just remember delays—they share them. Publicly. And virally.
- Employee fatigue—Agents forced to apologize for slow systems and bad processes burn out faster.
- Emotional defection—Even if the issue is eventually resolved, the emotional damage is done.

A Harvard Business Review study showed that reducing customer effort is a stronger driver of loyalty than delighting customers. Why? Because saving time saves trust. And when trust erodes, revenue follows.

Let's do the math. Imagine your contact center handles ten thousand calls a week. If each call contains three unnecessary minutes—repeating information, navigating menus, waiting for tools to load—you're wasting thirty thousand minutes a week. That's five hundred hours. Over a year, that's twenty-six thousand hours of wasted time. And that's just on the phone.

Now consider the ripple effect:

- Customers hang up and switch providers.
- Negative reviews spread on social media.
- CSAT scores decline.

- Employee morale drops.

Wasted time isn't a line item in your budget, but it's buried in every part of your P&L.

And in most organizations, no one owns it. Which means no one is fixing it.

The fix starts with recognizing time not as a cost of doing business, but as a product you deliver. Customers come to you for outcomes. But they stay—or leave—based on how long you take to deliver them.

Time is the one thing they won't forgive you for wasting.

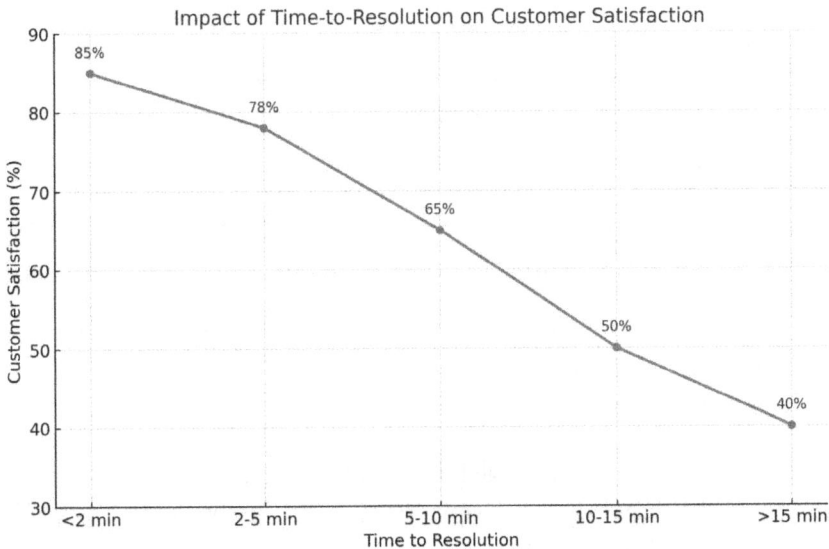

Impact of Time-to-Resolution on Customer Satisfaction

Source: Salesforce 'State of the Connected Customer' 2023; Gartner CX Trends 2023.

FRICTION IN EVERY CHANNEL

Time isn't just lost in long hold queues—it's lost in every channel customers touch. And when friction hides in plain sight, it's even more dangerous because it goes unaddressed.

On the phone: endless IVR menus, agents who ask for the same information multiple times, and transfers that go nowhere. One bank found that nearly 40 percent of calls were repeat contacts—not because the issue wasn't solvable, but because the customer gave up before it got there the first time.

In chat: bots that provide generic answers, or worse, trap users in loops. Many companies push chat as a "fast" option, but if it takes ten messages to connect with a person, the time advantage is gone. According to Zendesk, 54 percent of customers abandon chat when they feel they're not getting anywhere.

In email: Standard "we'll respond in forty-eight to seventy-two hours" replies are seen as unacceptable today. Customers expect asynchronous channels to move faster—especially for issues that impact billing, access, or fulfillment.

In apps: broken navigation, slow page loads, poor design. If a customer can't do what they need in three taps or less, they'll tap out. Data from Glassbox shows that 29 percent of mobile users who encounter friction in the first sixty seconds of a session abandon the task entirely.

In-store: clunky checkouts, long lines, confusing signage, or "I'm not sure, let me ask someone else" responses create drag even in physical locations.

Each of these moments—on their own—might seem minor. But when stacked, they become a system of delay that wears down trust and makes loyalty feel like a burden.

The worst part? Most of these delays are built by design. Policies made for internal efficiency. Tech decisions made without frontline feedback. Escalation protocols designed for risk avoidance, not resolution.

The customer feels every second of delay. Most companies don't even know it happened.

WHEN SELF-SERVICE BACKFIRES

Self-service isn't inherently bad. When it works, it's beautiful. A customer resets a password, files a claim, or updates an address in seconds—no call needed.

But when it fails, it's catastrophic.

The problem is too many self-service tools are designed around containment—not empowerment. They're built to keep customers out of live channels, not to solve problems quickly and clearly.

Think about the chatbot that can't recognize plain language and keeps asking the same questions. Or the portal that won't let you proceed without your exact account number—even though you're logged in. Or the knowledge base that looks robust, but gives vague, outdated answers.

These aren't rare cases. In a 2023 Gartner study, 70 percent of customers said they attempted self-service and still had to escalate to a human agent. Of those, nearly 60 percent said the process made them more frustrated than if they'd just started with a phone call.

The damage isn't just operational. It's emotional.

Poor self-service sends a clear message: "Figure it out yourself. But we're not going to make it easy."

True self-service respects time. It's intuitive. It's fast. It anticipates needs. Great self-service works so well that customers don't think of it as support at all.

Look at TurboTax: Their onboarding flow answers 90 percent of first-time user questions before a support session ever starts. Or Starbucks: Customers customize, pay, and pick up their drinks with minimal interaction—all because the app removes unnecessary steps.

Good self-service eliminates customer effort. Great self-service eliminates frustration.

When companies get this wrong, customers stop trusting digital. They go back to high-cost channels. And when that happens, your cost to serve spikes and satisfaction tanks.

If you want to protect both your bottom line and your brand reputation, don't just deploy self-service—design it like you mean it.

WHAT CUSTOMERS EXPECT NOW

Let's set a new benchmark—because the old one isn't good enough anymore.

Today's customers expect faster, simpler, and more seamless interactions than ever before. And they don't just expect it from one brand—they expect it from all of them. Whether they're ordering takeout, booking travel, applying for a mortgage, or seeking tech support, they expect every experience to be intuitive, responsive, and personalized.

According to Forrester:

- 77 percent of customers say valuing their time is the most important thing a company can do.
- 69 percent expect a response to a service inquiry within five minutes.
- 43 percent will walk away after a single poor digital interaction.

This is no longer about convenience. It's about survival. Customers don't give second chances for wasted time. They abandon the task, leave the brand, and rarely come back.

And speed alone isn't enough. Customers expect context. If they switch from a chatbot to a live agent, they expect the conversation to carry over. If they start an order online and finish it in-store, they expect continuity. If they already verified their identity in one channel, they don't want to do it again in another.

Omnichannel isn't a buzzword—it's a baseline. According to Salesforce's 2024 report, 82 percent of customers expect to solve complex problems by talking to one person. Yet more than half still report having to explain their issue multiple times.

And while expectations have risen, tolerance has shrunk. If your app crashes once, they might try again. If it happens twice, they delete it. If your support team misroutes them once, they may forgive it. If it happens again, they move on.

Customers want to feel like their time matters. That means giving them:

- Options that suit their lifestyle (chat, phone, app, email)
- Support that adapts to the complexity of their issue
- Systems that remember who they are and what they need

The companies that meet these expectations turn first-time users into loyalists. The ones who fall short create skeptics—fast.

THE DISNEY APPROACH: TURNING A WEAKNESS INTO A COMPETITIVE ADVANTAGE

If any company understands the true cost of customer waiting, it is Disney. In the realm of theme parks, where long lines are almost an accepted part of the experience, Disney has managed to turn waiting from a liability into a strategic asset. Decades ago, guests at Disney parks would spend nearly half of their day in line for rides, food, and attractions—a situation that not only diminished guest satisfaction but also cut into revenue.

Frustrated visitors spent less money, left the parks earlier, and were less likely to return. Recognizing this, Disney embarked on a mission to overhaul the entire waiting experience.

The transformation was multifaceted. One of the key innovations was the introduction of the FastPass system, which allowed guests to reserve specific ride times in advance. By staggering guest arrivals and managing peak periods more effectively, Disney was able to reduce congestion during busy times and create a smoother flow throughout the park. But Disney's innovations didn't stop at rides.

Real-time monitoring systems were put in place so that park employees could adjust operations dynamically, redirecting crowds from overloaded attractions to less crowded ones. This proactive approach not only shortened actual wait times but also reduced the perceived waiting time—an important psychological factor in customer satisfaction.

Additionally, Disney embraced mobile technology to further enhance the guest experience. With mobile ordering and payment systems, guests could bypass long queues at food counters, placing their orders through a dedicated app and picking up their meals without unnecessary delays. Even the waiting areas themselves were reimagined; some attractions introduced interactive queues that engaged guests with entertainment and information, transforming a period of idleness into a part of the overall experience. The results were striking higher guest satisfaction, increased in-park spending, and a notable uptick in return visits.

Disney's comprehensive approach to eliminating wait times stands as a testament to the fact that efficiency is not merely a matter of speed—it is about creating an experience that resonates with customers and leaves a lasting positive impression.

LEADERSHIP BLIND SPOTS - WHAT CX LEADERS AND EXECUTIVES MUST DO

The biggest threat to customer experience isn't a broken process or a bad interaction—it's a leadership team that doesn't see the full picture. Time is a strategic asset, yet many companies manage it like an afterthought. When leaders focus solely on what can be measured easily—like tickets closed, calls handled, or NPS movement—they miss the deeper truth: Customers leave not because things go wrong but because it takes too long to make them right.

And unlike traditional issues like product defects or pricing misalignment, time friction often slips under the radar. It hides between functions, disguised as standard process. It's normalized through years of internal approvals and legacy workflows. But for the customer, it doesn't feel like process—it feels like pain. It feels like disrespect.

Time is a strategic asset, yet many companies manage it like an afterthought. The root problem? Leadership blind spots.

While most senior leaders would never say, "We don't care about customer time," their org charts, systems, and decisions often say exactly that. The disconnect isn't usually due to apathy—it's due to assumptions. Assumptions that customers will tolerate delay. Assumptions that speed is someone else's department. Assumptions that CX can be measured in dashboards without understanding the stories behind the numbers.

FOR CX LEADERS: TELL THE STORY, NOT JUST THE SCORE

Let's bring it to life with an example. At one insurance provider, CX leaders discovered that policyholders calling to update their addresses were being bounced through three departments. It wasn't a malicious process—it had simply evolved over time. Each group owned a different database. By presenting a simple story—complete with the recorded customer call, a transcript, and a cost analysis of repeated touches—the CX team helped leadership understand how a three-minute fix was costing them tens of thousands of dollars a year in handling time and trust. That story led to a single-click update process that saved time and improved satisfaction overnight.

It's easy to rely on metrics. NPS. CSAT. Time to resolution. But numbers don't move hearts. Stories do.

The CX function must be more than a reporting engine. It must become the voice of the customer in the places where decisions get made. This means using real-world stories to humanize time delays and connect them to business impact.

- Don't just say "First response time is up." Show the story of a customer who waited eighteen minutes on hold, missed a delivery window, and took their business elsewhere.
- Don't just report repeat contacts. Tell the story of the parent trying to resolve a school-related payment with three kids in the backseat and no resolution in sight.

Leaders must also stop framing time as a service metric. It's a brand issue. A trust issue. A churn issue. If you don't advocate for time as a strategic priority, no one else will.

It's time to move beyond monthly scorecards and into the real business conversations—product roadmaps, resource planning, digital strategy. Time must have a seat at every one of them.

FOR C-SUITE LEADERS: STOP BURYING CX, START EXPERIENCING IT

Customer experience doesn't belong in a corner of the org chart. It belongs in the boardroom. Yet too often, CX is buried deep in marketing, siloed in operations, or split across functions with no singular accountability. That's not structure—that's neglect.

Let's be blunt: If your CX leader reports three levels down and has no budget, you've made a decision about how much the customer matters.

Executives who say they prioritize customers must prove it. That means:

- Elevating CX leaders to roles with budget and influence.
- Embedding CX metrics into the executive dashboard.
- Asking about friction points in operational reviews.
- Experiencing the journey firsthand—regularly.

If you're a CEO, when's the last time you tried to get a refund? Call your own IVR? Track a package through your app?

Leadership that stays too high-level creates blind spots. Blind spots become delays. Delays become churn.

And CFOs, take note: This isn't just about direct dollars on the P&L. CX is a long-term growth engine. Yes, reducing friction lowers cost to serve—but more importantly, great experiences drive lifetime value, lower acquisition costs, and build brand equity. Competence and speed generate referrals. Ease of service leads to product expansion. Treating CX as a soft ROI play misses the compounding impact it has across revenue streams.

When finance views CX through the same lens as product investment or sales enablement, everything changes. It becomes something to scale—not something to justify.

CX isn't just a service play. It's a growth lever. And it's time every C-suite leader acted like it.

The solution is proximity. Get closer to the problem. Talk to the front line. Sit in on customer calls. Shadow the live chat queue. Make decisions not just with data, but with empathy.

Because the customer doesn't feel your intent. They feel your process.

THE FIX: BUILDING A CULTURE OF URGENCY AND SIMPLICITY

If your customer says, "That was easy," you've already won.

But getting there takes more than good intentions. It requires architecture. Process. Culture. Most of all, it requires consistency.

Too many transformation efforts stall because they focus only on big initiatives. But the real leverage lies in the everyday decisions: the unnecessary approval, the outdated workflow, the overengineered policy.

Speed and simplicity must become your operating principles—not just talking points.

Below is a leadership checklist to begin building a time-respecting culture that scales.

Let's ground this with an example. At a global electronics firm, a newly formed 'Time Taskforce' reduced average call resolution time by 22 percent in just ninety days. They started by removing a mandatory agent wrap-up note that added thirty seconds per call. They then consolidated six IVR menus into one dynamic decision tree based on customer behavior. The changes weren't revolutionary. But they were relentless. And they worked. That's the power of a culture focused on time.

Time is too important to leave to chance. To build a culture that protects and prioritizes it, you need more than a memo. You need a playbook.

This isn't just about operations. It's a mindset shift. A leadership mandate. A CX strategy. And a long-term competitive advantage. It has to start with clarity, be reinforced by systems, and be modeled relentlessly at the top. Here's how to build it:

LEADERSHIP CHECKLIST

☑   Walk the journey yourself

Call your support line. Try to cancel a subscription. Return a product. Use your chatbot. When leaders live the customer experience, they don't need convincing to improve it.

☑   Redesign around the customer, not the org chart

Most delays aren't technology problems—they're structural ones. Handoffs between departments. Policies written for risk, not speed. Redesign processes around outcomes, not silos.

☑   Rethink your metrics

Track what customers actually feel: time to resolution, task-completion rate, and customer effort. Don't just count tickets—measure outcomes.

☑   Assign ownership for friction

Every delay should have a name next to it. Not a team. A person. Accountability speeds things up.

☑   Empower frontline teams

Give reps the tools and authority to resolve common issues without escalating. Faster resolutions. Lower costs. Happier customers.

☑   Audit and optimize self-service

Poor self-service is worse than none. Fix dead ends. Test journeys. Measure abandonment. Good self-service solves problems. Great self-service builds trust.

☑   Celebrate simplicity

Reward employees who find ways to make things easier. Add "time saved" to performance reviews. Make simplicity part of your brand DNA.

☑ Align experience with promise

Marketing can't promise "seamless" while operations deliver "slow." Make sure what you say externally matches what customers experience internally.

☑ Institutionalize urgency

Create a "Time Council" to regularly review top sources of delay. Set SLAs. Track outcomes. Drive action.

☑ Make time a core business value

Talk about it in town halls. Make it a board-level priority. When you treat time like money, your teams do too.

WHY TIME IS THE HARDEST THING TO WIN BACK

Time is the most unforgiving currency in customer experience. Once you waste it, you can't get it back. You can offer discounts, apologies, even gifts—but the clock doesn't rewind. And customers don't forget.

It's not just the literal minutes lost—it's the emotional tax it takes. It's the frustration of being transferred again. The irritation of having to repeat your story. The fatigue of waiting for a response to a question that should've had a quick answer. These moments erode trust one second at a time.

The challenge for most companies isn't that they don't care. It's that they don't prioritize. Time is often viewed as a resource to be managed internally—not an asset to be protected externally. But in the eyes of your customer, time is value. It's dignity. It's respect.

We are living in a post-convenience economy. Customers no longer reward you for being easy—they expect it. They don't notice when things go right; they only remember when it took too long.

And here's the part leaders often miss: Time compounds.

- The customer who had to verify their identity twice now assumes your systems are broken.
- The one who had to reexplain their issue on three channels no longer believes your team is competent.
- The one who waited five days for a refund now feels like they've been disrespected.

These small delays don't just hurt loyalty—they destroy it.

This is why time deserves a seat at every leadership meeting. Why it should be baked into product design, service strategy, and process reviews. Because time isn't a soft concept. It's a hard-edge business lever.

According to Bain & Company, companies that deliver a frictionless experience grow revenues 4 to 8 percent above their market. That's not marginal. That's meaningful. And it starts by valuing your customer's time as much as your own.

So ask yourself:

- Do we know where customers are losing time?
- Do we track time-to-value across journeys?
- Do we design for speed—not just resolution?

Because when you start measuring time as a trust metric, you start managing it differently. You become obsessed with removing the friction, collapsing the steps, and accelerating resolution.

And your customers notice. They remember.

In a world that moves faster every day, the companies that win aren't just the ones who respond quickly—they're the ones who respect time relentlessly.

Because time isn't just a differentiator. It's a dealbreaker.

And after all that effort? Customers still face another betrayal—unclear pricing, hidden fees, and charges that don't match the value they expected.

Key Takeaways

1. Every Extra Step Is a Message—and It's Usually "Figure It Out Yourself"

Customers don't judge your brand by how slick your tech is—they judge it by how easily they can get what they need. If they're navigating five clicks, two logins, and a call just to fix something you broke, they won't stay loyal. They'll stay frustrated—until they leave.

2. Effort Is the Hidden Tax in Every Customer Interaction

Every ounce of cognitive load—every confusing menu, dead-end chatbot, or repeated explanation—adds up. High-effort experiences don't just slow down resolution. They drain trust. And they cost you far more than the contact center budget shows.

3. Convenience at the Company's Expense Is a Short-Term Win and a Long-Term Loss

If your processes are designed to minimize cost for you while maximizing effort for the customer, you're building silent attrition into your model. The brands that win are the ones that solve for the customer, not through the customer.

CHAPTER 3

Hidden or Unexpected

THAT'S NOT WHAT YOU SAID IT WOULD COST

It started with what looked like a great deal. A couple booked a weekend getaway through a travel app advertising a luxury hotel at $189 per night. But when they checked out, the final bill was almost $270 per night. The breakdown? Resort fees. Facility charges. A "destination amenity" tax that included access to services they never used.

They felt duped. What started as excitement turned into resentment. They left the hotel disappointed, and by the time they left their review—complete with photos of the charges and a warning to future travelers—thousands had seen it. That post wasn't about the hotel anymore. It was about the betrayal.

This scenario isn't rare. Hidden fees are no longer exceptions—they're systemic. They've become so normalized that customers now brace for the final tally. Airlines, banks, telcos, apps, streaming services, and even grocery delivery platforms have all adopted layers of add-ons, fine print, and opt-outs that quietly inflate the cost of doing business with them.

But what these companies don't understand—or worse, choose to ignore—is that while those fees may pad short-term revenue, they erode long-term trust. And trust is much harder to recover than margin.

THE EROSION OF TRANSPARENCY

There was a time when pricing was a clear value exchange. You paid for something, and you got it. But over the past two decades, companies have added complexity in the name of flexibility, personalization, and profitability. The result? Customers often don't know what they're paying for until it's too late.

Hotels were early adopters of this model, quietly adding resort fees that cover things like Wi-Fi, pool access, or towel service—whether you use them or not. Airlines began unbundling their fares: bags, seat selection, overhead bin use, boarding priority—all add-ons now. Subscription services lure customers in with free trials and then bury the cancellation process under layers of clicks. Even restaurants have joined in, adding "kitchen appreciation" fees or "noncash adjustments" to the bill.

The justification? "Everyone else is doing it."

And that's the problem. The industry standard has become "acceptable opacity."

In a 2023 Consumer Reports study, 64 percent of Americans said they've encountered a hidden fee in the last year that significantly changed their willingness to do business with that company again. This isn't a pricing strategy—it's a trust tax.

WHAT IT FEELS LIKE TO BE TRICKED

From a spreadsheet perspective, a $7.99 convenience fee or a 12 percent service charge might seem negligible. But customers don't experience spreadsheets. They experience betrayal. They feel deceived, misled, and often embarrassed for not seeing it coming.

Being hit with hidden fees triggers what behavioral economists call a "loss of agency." It undermines a customer's feeling of control in the transaction—an experience that McKinsey research shows is critical to customer satisfaction and retention.

According to a 2023 Accenture report, 64 percent of consumers said unclear or unexpected charges made them question whether a company had their best interest at heart. And 48 percent said it made them less likely to recommend that brand to others.

This isn't just about perception—it's about identity. No one likes to feel duped. And when brands put customers in that position, it creates a permanent dent in the relationship.

That feeling is toxic. It changes how customers talk about you. It shifts the tone of reviews, the sentiment on social media, and the likelihood that they'll ever come back.

Psychologists refer to this as the expectation gap—the distance between what someone thinks will happen and what actually does. The wider the gap, the greater the emotional fallout.

When customers feel tricked, they rarely complain to the company. They complain to everyone else.

And once trust is broken, it's not just that customer you lose—it's everyone they influence.

WHERE HIDDEN FEES HIDE

Hidden fees don't always appear as line items. Often, they're camouflaged inside terms, processes, and assumptions that no longer reflect what today's customer expects—or tolerates.

Some industries are notorious for this practice:

- Travel & Hospitality: Resort fees, destination charges, energy surcharges, early check-in fees.
- Airlines: Seat selection fees, carry-on charges, credit card processing fees.

- Banking & Finance: Overdraft protection fees, minimum balance penalties, statement mailing charges.
- Telecommunications: Activation fees, device access fees, data overage charges.
- E-commerce & Delivery: "Service" charges, fuel surcharges, platform fees, nonrefundable tips.
- Subscription Services: Automatic renewals, upgrade traps, hidden tier restrictions.

They slip into:

- Checkout screens that delay total price visibility until the final step.
- Pop-up modals with fine print defaulted to "agree" status.
- Mobile app upgrades disguised as feature access.
- Post-purchase emails confirming additional charges the customer didn't authorize.
- Third-party platforms where the brand deflects responsibility to partners.

Even worse, these fees are often cloaked in vague, legal-sounding language designed to obscure rather than explain: "facility enhancement fee," "regulatory compliance adjustment," "convenience processing."

According to the Federal Trade Commission (FTC), hidden and junk fees cost US consumers billions annually—and erode market fairness by allowing less transparent companies to appear cheaper than they are.

Transparency isn't just good practice. It's a competitive differentiator—especially as governments around the world begin cracking down on deceptive practices and consumers grow more vocal and connected. Brands that stay ahead of transparency expectations won't just avoid backlash—they'll earn trust while others lose it.

THE DIFFERENCE BETWEEN VALUE AND GIMMICK

Customers are not opposed to paying for value. In fact, they're willing to pay more for clarity, control, and outcomes that feel worthwhile. But the line between value and gimmick is razor-thin—and most companies cross it without even realizing it.

What customers resent is being sold one thing and receiving another.

Take airline baggage fees. When a customer buys a ticket and then gets charged extra to bring a carry-on—something that used to be included— it feels like a bait-and-switch. But when Delta offers a bundled fare with additional perks clearly outlined, many customers will opt in—even if it costs more. The difference? One is opaque, the other is upfront.

Or consider subscription services. Customers will gladly pay for a streaming bundle that includes music, movies, and podcasts if the offering is cohesive and valuable. But when they're charged an "HD-streaming surcharge" on top of an already premium plan, the value proposition begins to unravel.

The psychology is simple: Customers want to feel in control. When pricing is transparent and additive, they perceive value. When it's obscured or forced, they feel manipulated.

According to PwC, 59 percent of consumers say transparency in pricing increases brand trust. Brands that communicate clearly—even when the cost is higher—tend to retain customers longer than those that bait with a low entry point and nickel-and-dime on the back end.

Customers aren't asking for cheap. They're asking for honesty.

Where Hidden Fees Damage Trust Most

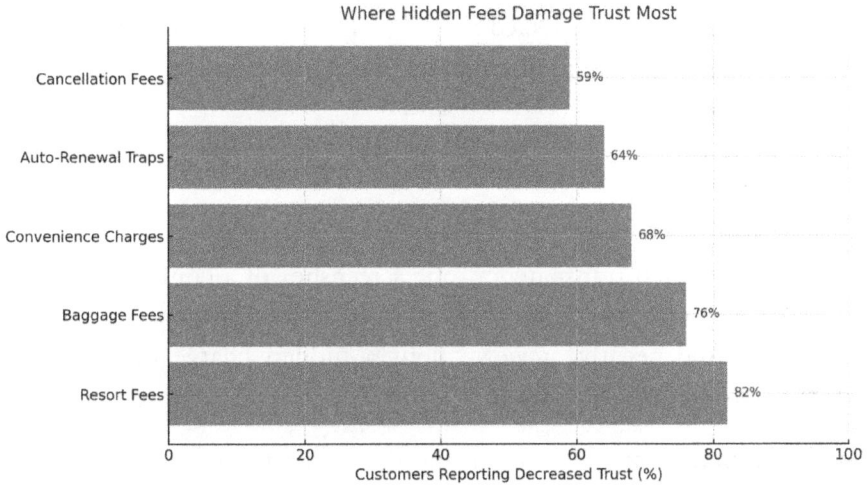

Source: Consumer Reports 2023; Pew Research; FTC Junk Fee Study 2023.

CUSTOMERS ARE SMARTER THAN YOU THINK

There was a time when brands could get away with obscure language and fine-print tactics. That time is over.

Today's customer research everything. They compare prices. They read reviews. They follow Reddit threads, TikTok explainers, and comparison blogs that dissect every clause of your pricing model.

They know when they're being tricked. And more importantly—they're willing to call it out.

Governments and consumer protection agencies are also responding to this shift.

- In the US, the Federal Trade Commission proposed new rules in 2023 aimed at banning "junk fees" across sectors, requiring companies to disclose full prices upfront.
- The UK's Competition and Markets Authority (CMA) launched investigations into online platforms using misleading pricing tactics, focusing particularly on drip pricing in travel and subscription services.

- Australia's ACCC (Australian Competition and Consumer Commission) has issued fines against telcos and retailers for failing to display total pricing, mandating transparency in all online advertising.

This global regulatory momentum sends a clear message: Pricing clarity is no longer optional.

In the age of digital transparency, one screenshot of a confusing bill can go viral. One influencer rant about a surprise fee can derail months of marketing. One negative review about a hidden charge can cost you dozens of prospective customers.

Smart companies are learning from this. They're publishing detailed FAQs. They're sending proactive messages that explain charges before they appear. They're empowering service teams to waive fees that weren't communicated clearly. Not as a favor—but as a policy.

Transparency is no longer a nice-to-have. It's a minimum requirement for trust.

And it's no longer just a CX issue. Legal, finance, marketing, product—all must align to ensure that what the customer sees is what the customer gets.

Because today's customer is not just smarter. They're louder. They're connected. And they're done being taken advantage of.

WHEN FEES BECOME THE STORY

In today's connected world, what used to be private frustration is now public spectacle. One hidden fee isn't just a personal annoyance—it becomes a headline, a meme, or a TikTok explainer. When fees cross the line from frustrating to absurd, they become the story.

Consider the infamous hotel "destination fee" scandal, where guests in Las Vegas and New York were charged over forty dollars per night for amenities like "access to the fitness center" or "local phone calls"—even if they never used them. Or the airline that added a thirty-five-dollar "carry-on bag fee," leading to social media backlash and coverage from major news outlets.

These moments do more than harm short-term reputation. They reshape perception. Customers don't just see the brand as greedy—they see it as untrustworthy.

A 2023 Deloitte study found that 57 percent of consumers say they would stop doing business with a company after just one experience they perceived as dishonest. And fees—especially when discovered after the purchase—rank among the top reasons for that perception.

Even worse, fee scandals have staying power. Customers might forget a minor delay or a clunky interface. But they remember when they felt taken advantage of—and they tell others.

Reddit forums are filled with screenshots of confusing invoices. YouTube creators make entire videos breaking down "junk fees" in car leases or ticket sales. Mainstream media now tracks and publishes rankings of brands with the worst fee transparency.

Once your pricing becomes the punchline, your brand becomes the warning label.

WHO'S RESPONSIBLE—MARKETING, LEGAL, PRODUCT, OR OPS?

Here's the real challenge: Hidden fees rarely start with bad actors. They creep into the business through silos. A product team wants to test monetization. Legal recommends protective language. Marketing promises simplicity, while ops focuses on internal workflows. Nobody means to erode trust—but it happens anyway.

That's why fee complexity is so hard to unwind. It isn't owned by one person. It's embedded into the seams of the business.

CX teams often flag the issue first—because they hear the complaints. But they don't own the fee structures. Product owns the pricing model.

Legal owns the language. Marketing owns the message. And operations owns the workflow.

This creates a diffusion of responsibility that enables bad practice to become standard practice.

The solution? Appoint a cross-functional owner of pricing transparency.

- Legal must approve clear language, not just compliant language.
- Product teams should test fee changes with real customers—not just analysts.
- Marketing must validate that messaging matches the actual experience.
- CX should advocate for clarity and be empowered to escalate deceptive practices.

When everyone owns part of the experience, no one owns the outcome. That's why trust breaks down.

To restore transparency, leadership must create accountability. Fee strategy isn't just a monetization lever. It's a brand-defining decision.

Because at the end of the day, the customer doesn't care who approved the fee. They only care that it showed up—and no one warned them.

A CALL TO ACTION FOR INDUSTRY LEADERS

For businesses seeking to thrive in today's competitive landscape, the path forward is unmistakable. It is no longer acceptable to rely on hidden fees as a revenue strategy. Instead, companies must embrace a new paradigm—one that places transparency, honesty, and respect at the center of every customer interaction.

Leaders must start by reassessing their pricing models and communication strategies. It is imperative to ask hard questions: Are all fees clearly disclosed before the customer commits to a purchase? Is the billing process simple and transparent? Does the company provide straightforward mechanisms for cancellation and subscription management? These questions are not mere operational concerns; they are strategic imperatives that directly affect customer retention and long-term profitability.

Moreover, a commitment to transparency should extend beyond pricing. It should permeate every aspect of the customer experience—from the clarity of product information to the ease of accessing customer support. When companies open up about their costs and processes, they invite customers into a relationship built on mutual trust and respect. This approach not only differentiates a brand from its competitors but also lays the groundwork for a loyal customer base that is more resilient in the face of market fluctuations and competitive pressures.

Fixing the fee problem isn't just about customer service—it's a leadership decision. And it requires two kinds of leaders working in tandem: CX advocates who elevate the voice of the customer, and executive leaders who model transparency from the top.

WHAT CX LEADERS MUST DO

CX leaders must see themselves not only as experience designers, but as organizational translators—converting customer pain into business imperatives.

CX leaders are often the first to hear the frustration. But they can't stop at listening—they need to bring the full story forward.

- Bring the data and the narrative. Don't just say "fees are frustrating." Quantify the volume of complaints, escalation rates, and churn correlation. Then humanize it with real customer examples.
- Audit the end-to-end journey. Know where pricing confusion lives—on the website, in the app, during the renewal. Capture screenshots, test flows, walk the customer path yourself.
- Be the connective tissue. Legal, product, ops, and marketing often work in parallel. CX leaders must convene them to build alignment.
- Push for proactive clarity. If fees can't be eliminated, they must be communicated early, clearly, and prominently.

- Champion customer time. Make time-to-value a central CX metric. Quantify delays. Show the lifetime value impact of speed versus friction.

- Close the loop. When fees are revised or removed, communicate the change back to customers. Let them know they've been heard—and respected.

Your job is not just to manage the experience. It's to be the organization's conscience—holding every department accountable to the customer's trust.

WHAT C-SUITE LEADERS MUST DO

The C-suite doesn't just approve pricing—they define the culture that allows it.

Executives must stop viewing transparency as a risk and start seeing it as a revenue multiplier. The data is clear: Customers stay longer with brands they trust—and they trust brands that are honest.

- Elevate CX to a strategic role. If your customer leader can't influence policy, they can't protect trust.

- Experience the pricing firsthand. Try buying your product or signing up for your service. If the process frustrates you, it's worse for the customer.

- Lead with transparency. Fees that feel hidden should be eliminated—or surfaced plainly. Customers don't expect everything to be free. They expect it to be fair.

- Challenge the CFO mindset. Not every fee needs to be defended in terms of immediate contribution margin. Some costs are offset by long-term loyalty and advocacy. Clarity builds retention. Fairness fuels referrals.

- Model zero tolerance for deception. The tone starts at the top. When executives speak out against shady fee structures, it gives the entire organization permission to challenge them too.

- Define and fund transparency as an initiative. If pricing transparency matters, it needs resourcing. Roadmap time.

Communications support. UX redesign. Treat it like product modernization or security—not a side project.

If trust is the currency of modern business, transparency is the exchange rate—and executives are its gatekeepers.

THE FIX: REBUILDING TRUST THROUGH PRICING TRANSPARENCY

The fix isn't easy—but it is simple. It requires intention, structure, and bold leadership. Transparency must stop being a campaign promise and start becoming a core part of how the business operates. It's not a marketing message. It's a design decision. It's a product decision. It's a leadership decision.

Treat transparency like a product. Design it. Test it. Measure it. Improve it.

- Start with language. Eliminate jargon. Use plain English. "Service charge" means nothing to the customer. "Credit card processing fee" does.

- Map the full pricing journey. How many clicks until the final price is visible? Is it consistent across devices? Is it the same before and after account creation?

- Create a pricing accountability team. One person—or group—must own the transparency mandate. Otherwise, it gets lost in the shuffle.

- Make fees optional where possible. Let customers opt into extras rather than forcing them.

- A/B test clarity. Try versions of your pricing page with and without breakdowns. See what builds trust—and what creates questions.

- Reward transparency. Celebrate teams who simplify and clarify. Feature them in town halls. Make clarity a KPI.

Transparency isn't a feature. It's a value. And it requires cross-functional ownership, regular inspection, and constant iteration.

Companies that get this right make transparency part of their culture. They empower teams to speak up when a pricing tactic feels misleading. They give service agents the ability to override a charge that wasn't clearly communicated. They bring customers into the process—asking them what they'd want to see, where they get confused, and what would help.

They build pricing that respects both intelligence and time. Because customers don't want handouts. They want honesty.

And when you live it out loud—through every screen, sentence, and service—you don't just rebuild trust.

You make it your competitive edge.

YOU CAN'T BUY TRUST BACK

Trust is a fragile thing. It takes months—sometimes years—to earn. But it can be lost in a single transaction. Especially when that transaction includes a fee the customer didn't see coming.

That's what makes hidden fees so dangerous. They don't just raise costs. They lower credibility. They tell your customer: "We want your money more than your confidence."

You can apologize. You can issue a refund. You can even remove the fee later. But the doubt lingers. The sense that the brand wasn't fully honest. And that erosion is hard to reverse.

In a 2023 KPMG study, 71 percent of consumers said they've stopped doing business with a company due to a lack of trust. And 55 percent said once trust is broken, it's unlikely they'll return—regardless of incentives.

Here's the reality: You can't market your way back into a customer's good graces after they feel deceived. You can't bribe your way to loyalty with points, perks, or promotions. Once a customer believes you've taken advantage of them, every future interaction is colored by that moment.

This is why pricing clarity isn't a tactical fix. It's a brand imperative.

Transparency builds trust. And trust builds everything else.

- It builds advocacy.
- It builds resilience when mistakes happen.
- It builds permission to raise prices—because the customer believes it's fair.

When customers know exactly what they're paying, and why, they don't just tolerate the price—they support it. And when they don't? They leave.

The companies that are winning today aren't the cheapest. They're the clearest. They've made honesty a business model. And in doing so, they've turned transparency into a competitive advantage.

So don't wait for your fee structure to go viral. Don't wait for regulators to force your hand. Don't wait for customer sentiment to slide into resentment.

Lead with transparency now—because trust is the one thing your customers won't give you twice.

But even when pricing is fair, trust unravels fast if the brand doesn't deliver on what is promised.

Key Takeaways

1. Surprise Fees Don't Just Frustrate—They Feel Like a Betrayal

When the final price doesn't match the promised price, customers don't see it as a misunderstanding. They see it as manipulation. Pricing transparency isn't a nice-to-have—it's foundational to trust.

2. Misleading Offers and Hidden Terms Turn Marketing into a Liability

If your fine print unravels your value proposition, you don't have a product problem—you have a credibility problem. Short-term gains from misleading offers lead to long-term churn and reputational damage.

3. Price Confusion Isn't Just a Sign of Complexity—It's a Sign of Misalignment

If customers frequently call to ask why they were charged a certain amount, that's not a billing issue—it's a signal that product, marketing, and CX are not aligned. Great companies price clearly, deliver consistently, and leave no one guessing.

CHAPTER 4

The Service Doesn't Work

A customer logs into their banking app at 7:45 a.m., trying to transfer funds before a payment hits their account. The app won't load. They try again. Still frozen. A third attempt sends them to an error screen.

Ten minutes later, the overdraft fee is applied.

The customer calls support and sits on hold for eighteen minutes. The rep can't see what happened and promises to "look into it" and "call back if there's an update." The call ends with no resolution, just a case number.

The customer doesn't just feel frustrated. They feel exposed. Like they trusted the wrong brand. Like the promise—twenty-four seven access, seamless digital banking, no surprises—was all marketing. They are thinking you didn't keep your promise.

And they're right.

But here's what's worse: This wasn't the first time. It had happened before—once during a travel emergency, once on a payday. And each time, the customer told themselves it was just a bug. Just a one-off. Just bad luck. Until it wasn't.

Now, the glitch became a pattern. The pattern became a story. And the story became their perception of the brand: unreliable, uncaring, incapable of delivering on even the simplest promise.

They post about the experience online. The post gains traction. Friends chime in with similar stories. Former customers share why they left. Prospective customers ask, "Is it really that bad?"

The post doesn't just reach their followers. It becomes a signal to the market. A case study in how brands lose customers not through one dramatic failure—but through one failure too many.

This is the moment most companies overlook: not when the product fails, but when the customer loses faith that it will work next time.

That's how broken experiences break trust. Not through the glitch itself, but through what the glitch reveals about the company's priorities, readiness, and commitment to reliability.

Because trust isn't about never failing. It's about what customers believe will happen the next time they need you.

They post about the experience online. And that post doesn't just reach their followers. It reaches future customers who now question the reliability of a service they've never even used.

How Service Failures Break Customer Trust

Service Failure	Customers Reporting Reduced Trust (%)
Repeated Downtime	66%
Failed Service at Critical Moment	74%
Missing Notifications	53%
Login Errors	59%
App Glitches During Payment	68%

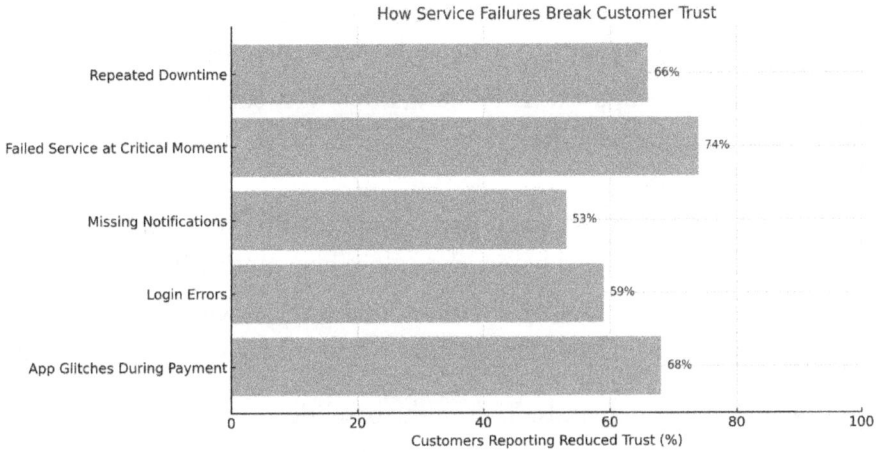

Source: Deloitte Digital 2023; Forrester CX Index; McKinsey 'Moments That Matter' Study, 2023.

WHAT CUSTOMERS EXPECT NOW

Customers don't just expect a product or service to work—they expect it to work every time, across every channel, without delay, without friction, and without needing to think about it. That's the bar now.

Today's customer expectations have been radically reshaped by the best digital experiences in the market. They expect the same from everyone—regardless of industry, size, or complexity.

- If Netflix loads instantly, they expect your video onboarding to as well.
- If Amazon lets them track packages in real time, they expect the same visibility from your support team.
- If a food delivery app shows real-time driver progress, they expect your tech to reflect basic order statuses.

According to a 2023 report from Deloitte, 82 percent of customers say the consistency of performance is more important to them than feature innovation. In other words, customers don't want bells and whistles—they want it to work, fast and flawlessly.

Here's what customers now assume:

- Cross-device performance: They expect your website, mobile app, and in-store systems to sync and behave identically.
- Always-on support: They want to contact someone when something breaks—on the channel of their choice, and without repeating their issue.
- Proactive updates: They don't want to discover problems. They want to be notified before the failure becomes their burden.
- Instant accountability: If something goes wrong, they want immediate resolution or escalation. No form. No queue. No excuses.

These aren't outlier demands. They're the baseline.

A Forrester study found that 65 percent of customers now rate digital experience as the most important part of their brand interaction—and 43 percent say they've stopped using a product or service entirely because it failed in a moment of need.

But here's the nuance: Customers aren't expecting perfection. They're expecting reliability with grace. If something goes wrong, they want it acknowledged, fixed fast, and prevented from happening again.

That means companies must evolve how they define success:

- It's not about availability alone. It's about responsiveness.
- It's not about uptime. It's about trust time—the confidence a customer has that what they see will work.

You don't need to be the fastest or flashiest. But you do need to be the most dependable.

Because reliability isn't just a tech spec. It's an emotional promise. One failure may be forgivable. Repeated friction? That's how relationships unravel.

GLITCH FATIGUE AND DIGITAL DISAPPOINTMENT

There was a time when customers were forgiving about digital flaws. Apps were new, systems were evolving, and bugs were expected. That era is over.

Today, customers are not only more reliant on digital products—they're exhausted by their failures.

Glitch fatigue is real. It's the frustration that builds when login screens freeze, checkout pages crash, or support chats fail to connect. It's the microaggressions of modern UX: buttons that don't work, alerts that arrive late, settings that won't save.

And it's cumulative. One glitch might be tolerable. Two gets annoying. But three? That's when the customer starts asking a deeper question: "Why am I still doing business with this company?"

This shift is driven by changing expectations. In a world where Google loads instantly, Uber updates in real time, and Spotify delivers curated playlists with zero lag, consumers now treat digital reliability as a given.

In a 2023 Capgemini report on digital experience, 74 percent of customers said they had zero tolerance for app crashes or repeated glitches, and 58 percent said they would uninstall an app after just two bad experiences. The same report found that consistent digital performance was the number one predictor of customer loyalty across retail, banking, and telecommunications.

Digital disappointment isn't always loud. Sometimes it's a silent exit. The user who stops logging in. The subscriber who lets their renewal lapse. The advocate who goes quiet. But in other cases, it's a broadcast event—tweets, reviews, Reddit posts detailing how the latest update ruined the experience.

And while companies rush to deploy new features, many fail to maintain what matters most: stability. In the pursuit of innovation, they overlook integrity.

Worse, when these glitches are normalized internally—when QA warnings are ignored or tickets are quietly closed without action—it signals to employees that customer friction is acceptable. That's how glitch tolerance turns into brand erosion.

Customers aren't expecting perfection. But they are expecting reliability. And when they don't get it, they don't just lose patience—they lose faith.

Because what the customer remembers isn't the clever onboarding flow or the gamified reward—they remember that it didn't work when they needed it most.

That's digital disappointment. And it's costing companies more than they realize.

THE COST OF FAILURE IN THE MOMENT THAT MATTERS

Not all failures are created equal. Some are mere inconveniences—annoying, but recoverable. Others strike in high-stakes moments, where reliability isn't just expected—it's essential. These are the moments that define whether a brand can be trusted.

Imagine trying to board a flight with a mobile ticket that won't load at the gate. Or submitting a loan application that crashes right before submission. Or relying on a health-monitoring app that fails to sync during a critical medical episode.

In these moments, the impact of failure isn't abstract—it's immediate, personal, and sometimes irreversible.

Consider the story of a mother trying to refill her child's asthma prescription through a health provider's mobile app. It fails during login. After trying the website, then calling a support line that routes her through four menus, she finally reaches someone—who says the prescription refill window closed an hour earlier. A digital failure became a medical risk.

In travel, a common scenario: A traveler arrives at a hotel late at night after a delayed flight. They open the app to confirm their reservation—but it's not there. The system didn't sync. The room was released. Now they're stranded, and the trust they had in the brand is erased by a single moment of breakdown.

According to a 2023 report from McKinsey, over 40 percent of consumers said they had experienced a digital failure during a critical transaction in the past six months. Of those, 73 percent said the failure significantly reduced their confidence in the brand's reliability.

And here's the real problem: Most companies don't even know these failures happened. They're buried in abandoned sessions, error logs, and unsubmitted support tickets. But the customer remembers.

What companies track as a "dropped session" or a "bug" is remembered by the customer as a broken promise.

It doesn't matter if the problem is fixed later. It matters that it failed when it was needed most.

That's what makes these moments so costly. Not just because of the churn they create—but because of the stories they generate. Stories about being stranded, delayed, disappointed, or dismissed.

When failure happens in the moment that matters, it doesn't just create inconvenience. It creates a reputation.

And that reputation spreads faster than any fix you can roll out the next day.

Brands spend millions trying to surprise and delight. But for most customers, what matters far more is this: Did it work?

Did the app load? Did the reservation process go through? Did the feature do what it promised, the first time, every time?

We live in an era of compressed expectations. Customers aren't comparing your experience to your competitors. They're comparing you to the best experience they've ever had—on any platform, in any industry. And in that world, reliability is the real luxury.

According to Salesforce's 2023 State of the Connected Customer report, 88 percent of consumers say trust in a brand hinges on consistently delivering on promises. And the most basic promise of all? That the product or service will work.

This isn't just about uptime. It's about dependability. Predictability. Confidence.

When something works consistently, customers don't think about it. They rely on it. But the moment it fails, the magic evaporates—and doubt takes its place.

Reliability is what turns one-time users into loyalists. It's what drives daily usage, word-of-mouth referrals, and customer stickiness. It becomes the invisible foundation of everything a brand hopes to build.

And when it's missing, no amount of promotional spin can fill the gap.

You can't delight your way out of broken.

According to Accenture's Global Consumer Pulse Research, 61 percent of consumers switched providers in 2023 due to a poor experience—many of them citing "unreliable service" as the root cause. And once customers leave, the cost to reacquire them can be five to ten times more than retaining them in the first place.

And yet, reliability is still treated as a back-end concern. A tech issue. A support ticket. Something to be patched instead of prioritized.

That's the blind spot.

Because the customer doesn't care where the problem originated. They only know that it happened on your watch—and it cost them time, money, or peace of mind.

When that happens too often, they stop calling support. They start shopping elsewhere. Worse, they start warning others to do the same.

WHY FIXING ISN'T ENOUGH

Fixing a failure may solve the problem, but it doesn't erase the experience.

Most companies believe that if they respond quickly, issue an apology, or credit an account, the customer will move on. And sometimes they do.

But often, the damage is already done—because recovery doesn't restore reliability. It merely patches the breach.

Customers don't judge brands by whether they can fix things. They judge them by how often things break—and how often they have to ask for help in the first place.

In a 2023 Gartner study, 79 percent of consumers said they remember the emotion they felt during a service failure more than the resolution itself. When trust is compromised, even a flawless recovery can't undo the initial letdown.

Think of it like a bridge collapse. Fixing the bridge matters. But what the community remembers is that they couldn't get where they needed to go. That sense of insecurity doesn't go away overnight.

Fixing puts out the fire. But prevention builds trust.

When customers are forced to navigate recovery flows, submit support tickets, or sit on hold after something breaks, they begin to question the overall integrity of your brand. They don't want apologies. They want assurance it won't happen again.

Too many companies pour energy into polishing the recovery script instead of eliminating the root cause. They build impressive refund flows while failing to address the systems that cause failure in the first place.

Recovery is not the brand moment you want to optimize. Resilience is.

The brands customers trust the most are the ones they rarely need to call. The ones that anticipate, prevent, and resolve quietly—before the customer ever notices.

If a failure occurs and your first instinct is to ask, "How do we make this right?"—you're already late. The better question is: "How do we make sure this never happens again?"

Because at some point, fixing stops being appreciated—and starts becoming expected. And when that expectation sets in, you're no longer a trusted brand. You're just another one they're preparing to leave.

COMPANIES GETTING IT RIGHT

Reliability isn't luck. It's leadership. The brands that deliver consistent, dependable experiences do so by design. They invest in systems, empower their teams, and build cultures where quality is nonnegotiable.

Take Apple, for example. Their reputation for product reliability isn't just about hardware. It's about the seamless experience—how the software and support work together to reduce friction. Updates are stable. Repairs are fast. Support agents have tools that work. As a result, Apple consistently tops customer satisfaction rankings not just in electronics—but across all industries.

Toyota has long been known for its focus on continuous improvement, or "Kaizen." But what makes their reliability legendary is how that philosophy shows up in the product. Vehicles aren't rushed to market. Components are tested to failure. Quality control is embedded in every factory, every supplier, every tier of design. It's not glamorous. But it's effective. And it's why Toyota earns more repeat buyers than most automakers.

American Express is another brand that wins not with price—but with trust. Their customers know that when a transaction goes wrong, the company makes it right—quickly, and without hassle. Behind the scenes, this is enabled by an integrated system that connects data across service, risk, and product. The customer doesn't see the machinery—but they feel the result.

More recently, Spotify has become a case study in digital consistency. While not perfect, their streaming platform delivers personalized content across devices with minimal latency or drop-off. When outages do occur, they're acknowledged publicly and resolved rapidly. That transparency and consistency keeps users loyal even as competitors flood the market.

What do these companies share?

- They prioritize system stability over feature bloat.
- They empower frontline teams to resolve issues without red tape.

- They measure success not just by what launches—but by what lasts.
- They treat reliability as a brand promise—not a back-end function.

And here's what's most important: Their reliability isn't reactive. It's proactive. It's institutionalized.

In a 2023 Bain & Company report, companies that ranked highest in operational reliability saw customer lifetime value 1.6 times higher than their industry peers. Because when the product works, the customer stays.

Customers don't reward reliability with applause. They reward it with loyalty. With silence. With trust.

And that's the ultimate goal. Not to fix everything instantly. But to build systems, cultures, and brands that rarely need to.

Leadership Accountability for Product Reliability

When things break, fingers point. It was a system issue. A vendor update. A product oversight. An engineering bug. But to the customer, it doesn't matter who owns the fix. What matters is that it failed—and nobody seemed prepared.

Reliability is everyone's job. But leadership defines whether it becomes everyone's priority.

For many companies, product reliability is treated as a technical function. It's scoped into sprint plans, delegated to engineering, or filed under QA. That mindset misses the bigger truth: When your product fails, it's not just a tech failure—it's a trust failure. And recovering that trust is a business-wide responsibility.

Great brands don't silo reliability. They elevate it.

Product teams own performance—but they also own communication. If an issue arises, are customers notified? Are expectations reset? Or does silence send a different message?

CX teams must translate issues into stories. Not bug reports. Stories. This is what broke. This is who it affected. This is how it made them feel. This is what they did next. These stories build urgency in ways dashboards cannot.

Operations teams must track not just cost, but impact. What's the churn delta after a failure? What's the increase in support contacts? What's the revenue risk from lost transactions or delayed usage?

And most importantly, executive leaders must champion reliability not just as a checkbox, but as a competitive advantage.

- Are reliability KPIs visible in leadership reviews?
- Are service disruptions addressed openly and fast?
- Is tech debt being paid down proactively—or ignored in favor of short-term gains?

Accountability doesn't mean blame. It means clarity. Every layer of the business should know what part of the customer's confidence they are responsible for protecting.

Amazon's leadership famously includes a seat for the customer in key meetings—symbolically and practically. It's a reminder that someone is depending on what they build to simply work.

That mindset is the hallmark of reliability-focused organizations. They audit before issues arise. They listen to frontline employees. They build fail-safes, not workarounds. And they make reliability a product feature—not just an operational outcome.

Because customers may not know how your systems work. But they know when they fail. And if your leadership doesn't take ownership of that moment—you'll own the consequences.

THE FIX: BUILD IT RIGHT, PROVE IT WORKS, OWN THE GAPS

Too many companies treat reliability as something that happens behind the curtain—out of sight, managed by technical teams, and addressed only when something breaks. But in the customer's world, reliability is always center stage. It's what makes them come back, refer friends, and invest long-term trust in a brand.

So how do you fix it?

You build it right. You prove it works. And you own the gaps when it doesn't.

Build it Right

Reliability must be designed into the product—not bolted on afterward. That means:

- Designing for failure by anticipating common stress points and having safeguards in place.
- Simplifying architecture to reduce complexity and avoid cascading errors.
- Embedding QA upstream, not just at the end of development.

But it goes beyond technical design. Developers must understand how customers actually use the product—not just how it's supposed to function. They should know what problem the product solves, what journey the customer takes, and where the friction points are. Building it right means building it intuitively. It means putting usability and real-world behavior ahead of feature ambition.

Bring customer insights into sprint planning. Involve frontline staff in design reviews. Ask those who speak with customers daily what breaks most often—and why. The best-performing teams don't just write great code. They write for real-world context.

Reliability isn't just a testing function. It's a design philosophy. And design starts with empathy.

PROVE IT WORKS

Assumptions are the enemy of reliability. Just because a product launches doesn't mean it performs. That's why great companies test obsessively—not just in the lab, but in the real world.

- Monitor uptime across all platforms, including APIs and third-party integrations.
- Track usage patterns to identify bottlenecks or friction before customers hit them.
- Use synthetic testing and load simulations to validate performance under real-world conditions.

But proving it works requires going further. Don't launch a new feature until you've tested it from the customer's point of view—start to finish. Have real employees use the product like a real customer would. Involve support agents, sales reps, or frontline staff in the final mile of QA. They know how customers behave better than most developers do.

Run usability tests. Walk through the full experience on slow Wi-Fi. Try it on old phones. Proving reliability doesn't mean ticking off test cases—it means proving that the product holds up in real life, under real pressure, by real people.

Because if your team only validates what's supposed to work, you'll miss what's actually breaking trust.

OWN THE GAPS

When things break—and they will—it's not just about fixing fast. It's about who steps forward and takes responsibility.

- Acknowledge the issue early and clearly.
- Notify impacted users with transparency and empathy.
- Offer resolution proactively—not reactively.

Owning the gap means saying, "We got this wrong, and here's how we'll make it right." It's not just a customer service script—it's a leadership act.

For CX leaders, this means closing the loop. Not just solving the issue, but reporting it back to the organization with clarity and urgency. Document the fallout. Capture the root cause. Amplify the customer voice.

For the C-suite, owning the gap means showing up. When a high-profile failure happens, does leadership hide behind press releases? Or do they personally reinforce the values of transparency and accountability? Companies like JetBlue and Delta have had senior leaders directly acknowledge system failures during outages—and customers noticed.

Owning the gaps means executive ownership. Not just funding the fix, but modeling the response. When your CEO or COO treats service failures as business failures—not just ops issues—it signals that reliability matters from the top down.

Because when leaders take the hit, customers give them credit. And when they don't, customers write them off.

The best companies don't just manage outages. They build goodwill during them—and long after.

And beyond incident response, they institutionalize the lessons:

- Postmortems that include CX and comms, not just engineering.
- Shared learning repositories that prevent the same issue from repeating.
- Executive attention to root causes, not just incident logs.

Reliability doesn't scale through optimism. It scales through obsession.

The fix isn't just technical. It's cultural. It requires shifting from a "fix it when it breaks" mindset to a "prove it will hold" standard. It means removing the friction before the customer ever feels it.

Because when you build it right, prove it works, and own the gaps—you're not just delivering a better experience.

You're earning the right to be trusted.

CRAFTING A CULTURE OF RELIABILITY

At the heart of every digital service is the promise of reliability. It is not enough to simply avoid major failures; companies must cultivate a culture where stability and customer experience are ingrained in every process.

This begins with a fundamental shift in mindset: from viewing technology as a temporary tool to embracing it as the backbone of your brand. When every department, from development to customer support, is aligned with the goal of delivering a seamless, dependable service, the entire customer experience is elevated.

Leadership plays a critical role in fostering this culture. Executives must champion quality over speed and invest in the systems and people necessary to ensure that every aspect of the service functions as promised.

Regular reviews of system performance, customer feedback, and support outcomes should be standard practice. When failures occur—and they inevitably will—the focus should be on rapid learning and continuous improvement rather than deflection or denial.

THE BOTTOM LINE: RELIABILITY IS NONNEGOTIABLE

In today's digital economy, the promise of a service that "just works" is paramount. Customers have little tolerance for glitches, delays, or unresolved issues. Every time a service fails to deliver on its promise, the customer's trust is chipped away, sometimes irreparably. Whether it's a mobile banking app that crashes during a simple transfer, a video streaming service that buffers incessantly, or an online platform that fails to process orders, the effect is the same: Customers walk away, and they rarely return.

The brands that succeed are those that obsess over reliability, that anticipate potential failures, and that respond with speed and transparency when issues do arise. Reliability is not just a feature—it is the very foundation of customer trust and long-term loyalty.

The journey to excellence in customer service demands that every interaction, every transaction, and every digital experience is reliable. It means committing to quality at every level, from development and testing to customer support and incident management. When customers see that a company takes their experience seriously—when they witness proactive measures to prevent failures and swift action to correct them—they are more likely to forgive occasional missteps and remain loyal in the long term.

In the end, if your service doesn't work, customers will walk away, and they won't hesitate to share their frustrations with the world. The brands that will thrive in the digital age are those that understand that reliability is nonnegotiable and that every failure is an opportunity to rebuild trust through honest communication and effective resolution.

Welcome to the era where consistency, stability, and swift, empathetic responses are the cornerstones of customer service. In this landscape, every technical success is a testament to your commitment to excellence, and every resolved failure reinforces the trust that is essential to lasting customer relationships.

The question remains: Will your company be known for a seamless, dependable service that meets customers' needs at every turn, or will it be remembered as yet another brand that overpromised and underdelivered? The choice is yours, and the time to act is now.

Key Takeaways

1. The Bigger the Promise, the Bigger the Fallout

Marketing sets the expectation. CX delivers on it. When there's a gap between what was promised and what actually happens, customers don't downgrade their expectations—they downgrade their trust.

2. Brand Credibility Lives in the Gap Between Hype and Experience

Customers don't care what your slogan says if their package is late, their upgrade is broken, or the premium service feels generic. Every disconnect chips away at brand equity.

3. Failure to Deliver Isn't Always the Problem—It's How You Respond When You Do

Mistakes happen. But when a company acts surprised by failure, blames the customer, or hides behind process, they're no longer in the business of service—they're in the business of self-preservation. Recovery begins with ownership.

CHAPTER 5

Billing Issues

A customer logs in to cancel a subscription service they no longer use. They've already gone through the cancellation process once. Or so they thought. A month later, another charge appears. They check their account, which now shows no record of the earlier cancellation. Confused, they call support. The agent, reading from a script, informs them the cancellation didn't go through because they didn't receive a confirmation email—and without it, the system automatically reenrolled them.

Now the customer is being charged for a service they don't want, can't use, and already attempted to cancel. Worse, the refund request is denied due to "policy."

The amount? Less than twenty dollars. But the frustration? Immense.

They post about it online—screenshots, timestamps, and all. Others chime in: "That happened to me too." Dozens more recount similar experiences. The company didn't just lose one customer—they lost dozens of prospects who witnessed what looked like a scam in plain sight.

This is the tipping point most companies miss. Not when the charge happens, but when the customer is forced to chase their own money. When your billing process feels like a trap, your reputation becomes collateral damage. Customers shouldn't have to fight for their own money.

Because in a world where trust is currency, nothing bankrupts it faster than making your customer feel robbed.

And that's exactly what's happening in too many companies today—not through malice, but through neglect. Through fragmented ownership, opaque policies, and billing systems designed for the business, not the customer.

This chapter explores the toll of broken billing systems, the emotional and financial damage they inflict, and why fixing them isn't just good practice—it's a leadership imperative.

Some of the worst offenders span industries that touch millions daily:

- Telecommunications, where confusing bundles, overage charges, and hard-to-cancel contracts are industry norms.
- Airlines and Travel, with fees for baggage, seat selection, and re-booking that are often hidden until the final click.
- Subscription Streaming Services, notorious for auto-renewal traps, misleading trial offers, and unclear cancellation flows.
- Health Insurance, where explanation-of-benefits statements rarely match the bills, and navigating charges feels like decoding a puzzle.
- Hospitality, especially hotels and resorts, where "resort fees" and parking surcharges often show up post-booking.

These aren't isolated issues. They've become systemic habits—practices that erode trust even in well-known brands. And as customers grow more aware, more vocal, and more empowered, companies can no longer afford to dismiss billing as a back-office detail.

The cost isn't just operational. It's reputational.

How Billing Issues Undermine Customer Trust

Category	Customers Reporting Decreased Trust (%)
Denied Refunds (Policy-Based)	66%
Confusing Invoices	61%
Incorrect Charges	69%
Refund Delays	72%
Auto-Renewal Without Notice	78%

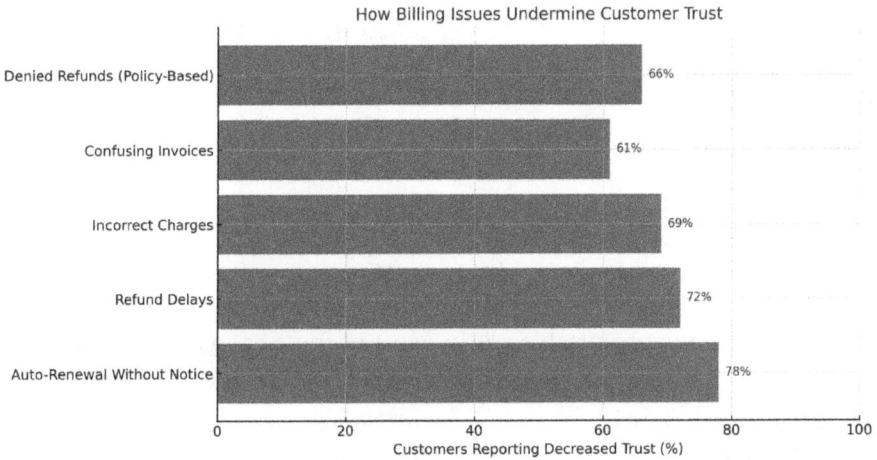

Source: PwC 2023 Customer Trust Study; Salesforce Connected Customer Report; Accenture 2023 Consumer Pulse.

THE HIDDEN TOLL OF BROKEN BILLING

When a customer is overcharged—even by a few dollars—the financial impact may be small, but the emotional response is often disproportionate. That's because billing touches something deeper than dollars: It touches trust. Customers expect brands to honor their side of the financial agreement. When that breaks down, the experience becomes personal.

The real damage isn't just in the refund or the lost transaction—it's in the friction, the effort, and the resentment it creates.

According to a 2023 PwC study, 65 percent of consumers say billing issues are one of the top three reasons they stop doing business with a company. And a Salesforce report from the same year found that 71 percent of customers say the way a company handles billing reflects how much it respects them.

When customers are forced to chase their own money—filing support tickets, repeating their story, and navigating opaque policies—they begin to feel not just ignored, but exploited.

It's not just a CX issue. Broken billing systems flood customer service channels with avoidable volume. They increase average handle time, frustrate agents, and strain internal resources. What looks like a revenue-generating operation becomes a cost center in disguise.

And then there's the reputational cost. A billing complaint that once stayed between the customer and the brand now plays out on social media, review sites, and forums. One viral post can undermine years of brand equity.

Billing errors don't just create disputes. They create distrust.

And here's the uncomfortable truth: Most of these errors are self-inflicted. They're not the result of fraud or malice—but of misaligned priorities, overengineered policies, and poorly integrated systems. In many cases, the billing process is overly complicated not because it needs to be, but because no one ever stopped to simplify it. Companies deploy a complex tech stack for subscription, payments, and invoicing—without connecting it to the broader customer journey. What results is a billing experience built around internal requirements, not external clarity.

Opaque terms, hidden clauses, and passive design choices force customers into a system that requires constant vigilance. And most customers don't have the time—or desire—to audit every charge. That's what makes these failures so dangerous. They often go unnoticed until frustration boils over.

Transparency isn't just about legal disclosures. It's about designing billing flows that assume the customer deserves simplicity, not suspicion.

That distrust lingers long after the refund is processed. Because when money is involved, customers remember the inconvenience, the emotion, and the sense that they had to fight for fairness.

That's a scar—not just a mistake. And it doesn't fade quickly.

In the chapters ahead, we'll examine why billing problems persist, who really owns the process, and what leaders must do to make sure customers never have to ask for what they're owed.

WHY CUSTOMERS FEEL CHEATED

Customers don't just feel frustrated when a billing issue occurs—they feel deceived. It's not just the financial inconvenience, it's the message it sends: You weren't paying attention, or worse, you were hoping they wouldn't.

Billing is deeply emotional. When a customer gives you their payment details, they're extending trust. They're saying: "I believe you'll be honest, accurate, and fair." So when a charge appears unexpectedly—or a refund never comes—it doesn't feel like a mistake. It feels like a betrayal.

And betrayal is remembered.

In a 2023 Accenture study, 70 percent of consumers said billing errors made them question the overall integrity of a company. It's not just about the charge—it's about what that charge represents: carelessness, misalignment, or greed.

It's particularly offensive when the burden of resolution falls on the customer. When they must call, email, screenshot, and argue to get back what was rightfully theirs, the experience becomes punitive. They feel punished for trusting you.

And the effort required to fix the mistake only deepens the wound. Customers are often forced into a scavenger hunt just to prove their case—digging up transaction IDs, sending screenshots, tracking down confirmation emails, or escalating through multiple layers of support. They wait days for follow-ups, repeat their story to every new representative, and are sometimes told, "There's nothing we can do."

This burden is especially infuriating because the customer didn't create the problem. The company did. Yet the resolution process treats them like the one at fault. The more hoops they have to jump through, the more the experience feels like a designed inconvenience—a tactic rather than an error.

And in many cases, the only resolution offered is a credit or a vague apology, rather than a real commitment to fix the root issue. Customers aren't just looking for their money back—they're looking for accountability.

They want acknowledgment that the mistake wasn't theirs. They want to know it won't happen again.

When that's missing, it's not just poor service—it's reputational erosion in real time.

These reactions aren't dramatic—they're logical. Because to the customer, if you can't get billing right, what else are you getting wrong?

Every billing failure is a trust withdrawal. And repeated failures? That's how customers feel you've stolen from them—not just financially, but emotionally.

That's why customers don't just leave. They leave loudly. And they take others with them.

WHAT BILLING FAILURES SIGNAL TO THE CUSTOMER

A billing error may look like a small glitch from the company's perspective, but to the customer, it signals something deeper. It tells them the company isn't in control of its own systems. That the organization doesn't value their time or money. That accuracy is optional—and accountability is negotiable.

And those signals add up.

To a customer, a broken billing experience can signal:

- Internal dysfunction. If you can't charge or refund correctly, what other systems are failing behind the scenes?
- A lack of care. Customers think, "If this was happening to your CEO, would it still be broken?"
- A deliberate tactic. Especially when patterns emerge, customers begin to suspect the confusion is by design.
- A breakdown in priorities. The perception becomes: This company cares more about protecting revenue than protecting relationships.

When billing goes wrong, the customer starts to reevaluate the entire relationship. They begin looking at every charge more skeptically. They hesitate before upgrading or referring a friend. They're no longer an advocate—they're a skeptic.

Even more damaging, these moments often override positive experiences.

You can build the best product in your category—a beautifully designed interface, lightning-fast features, and seamless onboarding—but a billing misstep can unravel it all in seconds. Because no matter how good the product is, if the customer feels financially manipulated or inconvenienced, their memory of your brand is rewritten. The glitch isn't remembered. The surprise charge is. The intuitive workflow doesn't get praised. The billing fight does.

This is especially true in industries where the product experience is high-touch and emotionally driven, like fitness, travel, entertainment, and digital services. A customer might rave about a travel app's booking interface—until they get charged twice for the same reservation. At that moment, the app is no longer "easy and convenient." It's "deceptive and unreliable."

Billing is the closing loop of the customer experience. If that loop is broken, the rest of the journey is invalidated. A great product, a thoughtful interaction, a smooth onboarding—all of it is eclipsed by the sting of feeling financially disrespected.

This is the multiplier effect of poor billing: One misstep doesn't just cost a refund—it rewrites the narrative.

So while billing may live in finance or IT or operations, its failure is felt across the brand.

Because when money is involved, customers assume the worst. And if you don't make it right, they're not just gone—they're vocal, influential, and far more likely to dissuade others from ever trusting you. They leave loudly. And they take others with them.

WHO OWNS BILLING (AND WHY THAT'S A PROBLEM)

Billing doesn't live neatly in one department. It's a spiderweb—touched by finance, product, technology, legal, marketing, and customer service. And in most companies, that means no one truly owns the full billing experience. Everyone owns a piece. But no one owns the outcome.

Finance owns the logic and revenue recognition. Product manages the interface and payment flows. Legal writes the fine print. Tech integrates the systems. CX handles the fallout. And marketing... well, marketing promotes a frictionless experience that billing often doesn't deliver.

This fractured ownership leads to gaps. Gaps in policy clarity. Gaps in accountability. Gaps in common sense.

When a billing error occurs, who reviews it end to end? When a refund policy is creating churn, who escalates it and fixes the wording? When a subscription auto-renews without notice, who asks if that's the experience the brand really wants to deliver?

The answer, too often, is no one.

Even worse, the tools and teams that manage billing are rarely aligned. The billing software may have been selected by procurement. The payment processor by IT. The refund approval flow by finance. The customer doesn't care who made the decisions—but they feel every one of them when things go wrong.

And so, small billing issues become chronic pain points. CX hears them but can't fix them. Finance defends the policy. Legal avoids risk. And the customer is left paying the price—not just with money, but with time and trust.

What's needed is a single owner of billing experience. Someone accountable not for the spreadsheets, but for the sentiment. Someone who reviews billing flows with the same rigor applied to user journeys. Someone who asks, "Would this make sense if I were the customer?"

This leader doesn't need to live in finance or customer service—but they must have the authority to work across them. They need the ability to redesign how billing operates—not just from a process standpoint, but from a trust standpoint.

Because without that, billing becomes a black box. Customers are told, "That's just how the system works." But no one is questioning why it works that way—or whether it should.

When billing lacks ownership, it lacks empathy. And when it lacks empathy, it becomes a silent churn engine that damages loyalty long before leadership even sees the impact.

THE CX AND C-SUITE LEADERSHIP BREAKDOWN

If billing is broken, the customer doesn't blame the back-end system or third-party vendor. They blame the brand. And when no one inside the company owns that experience end to end, customers are left paying the price—literally.

This is where the disconnect between CX leadership and the executive suite becomes dangerously obvious.

On the front lines, CX teams see the fallout every day. Support agents field refund requests, try to explain complex billing logic, and deal with angry customers who feel tricked. And often, they're doing it without access to accurate or up-to-date billing data. In many organizations, frontline teams must navigate outdated systems, disconnected platforms, or buried policy documents just to verify a charge—let alone resolve it. They're expected to serve as the face of resolution while being starved of the tools and information they need to truly help. That lack of enablement doesn't just frustrate the customer—it demoralizes the employee. Yet often, those same teams have no influence over the billing system, the policies behind it, or the language customers see. They're responsible for cleaning up a mess they didn't make.

Meanwhile, the C-suite may never experience what it's like to dispute a charge with their own company. Billing is often buried in finance or IT, with no clear ownership from anyone accountable for the customer journey. There's no executive walking the billing experience from end to end and asking: "Would I be okay with this if it happened to me?"

AND THAT'S THE PROBLEM.

When executives don't see billing as a customer experience issue, it never gets prioritized. It doesn't show up in the CX scorecard. It doesn't receive funding for redesign. It doesn't get fixed.

The result? Customers deal with billing errors that look like scams, policies that sound like excuses, and systems that feel like they're designed to fail.

Leadership isn't about having all the answers—it's about being accountable for the experiences your customers are having, whether they're intentional or not. And when it comes to billing, too many senior leaders remain disconnected from what customers actually go through.

That disconnect costs more than money. It costs trust.

If you're not experiencing your own billing flows, if your CX leader can't escalate a pattern of complaints to someone who can fix the root cause, and if finance is more concerned with policy enforcement than customer retention—then you've already lost control of the narrative.

Billing is not just a transaction. It's a trust moment. And if leadership isn't owning it, customers will assume the company doesn't care.

And they won't stick around to find out who does.

COMPANIES GETTING IT RIGHT

Some companies have cracked the code on billing. Not just by avoiding errors—but by turning the billing experience into a trust-builder, not a liability.

Take Spotify, for example. Their subscription management process is simple, clear, and forgiving. Users can cancel, downgrade, or change payment methods with just a few clicks—no games, no guilt, no "call us to cancel." When a billing issue occurs, Spotify is quick to acknowledge it, offer resolution, and make it right without hiding behind red tape.

Chewy, known for their customer-first ethos, handles billing issues with empathy and speed. If a pet parent is mistakenly charged or a subscription shipment goes out too soon, Chewy's support team has both the authority and information to correct it immediately. Refunds are issued proactively, and the messaging is apologetic, not defensive. That kind of transparency doesn't just solve the problem—it reinforces loyalty.

In financial services, American Express continues to lead with a service model that sees billing disputes as opportunities to earn trust. Their teams are trained not just to issue credits, but to ensure the customer understands the resolution. Billing accuracy is treated as an extension of brand reputation, not just an accounting function.

Then there's Apple, which has built refund simplicity into its digital ecosystem. If a customer is accidentally charged for an app or service, they can request a refund directly from their purchase history—no support call required. The process is so clean that it feels intentional, not reactive.

What do these companies have in common?

- Clear ownership of the billing experience.
- Proactive, not reactive, approaches to communication.
- Empowered frontline teams with access to accurate billing data.
- A cultural understanding that trust is earned in the details.

They don't just issue refunds. They remove the need for them.

Consider brands like Amazon and Zappos. These companies are lauded for their proactive approach to returns and refunds—not because they process returns, but because they make the refund experience effortless. In many cases, customers receive a refund as soon as tracking shows the return is in transit—not after it's received or inspected. That kind of speed and trust signals, "We believe you."

There's no three to five business day waiting period. There's no extended approval window. These brands understand that if the customer made the effort to return an item, delaying their refund only introduces friction. Instead, they front-load the goodwill. And that gesture goes further than any loyalty discount ever could.

Companies that lead in billing have made one simple commitment: If we're fast to charge you, we'll be just as fast to credit you. That kind of symmetry creates a sense of fairness customers don't forget.

And in doing so, they turn billing—a source of stress in most companies—into a brand advantage in theirs.

SO WHY DO THEY GET IT RIGHT?

Because they understand what's at stake. These companies know that billing is not just about revenue capture—it's about relationship maintenance. Every charge, credit, and cancellation is a brand interaction. And the smoother that experience is, the more trust they earn.

They've recognized that a customer who trusts their billing experience will:

- Spend more confidently,
- Subscribe more willingly,
- Stay loyal longer,
- And refer friends without hesitation.

They get it right because they've felt the pain of getting it wrong. They've listened to customer backlash, read the angry reviews, and felt the financial and reputational cost of friction.

Most importantly, they've elevated billing from a back-end function to a strategic asset. They've asked hard questions: What does our billing say about our brand? Are we making it easy to trust us? Are we treating every payment like a moment of service?

They know that clarity breeds confidence. That transparency builds loyalty. And that simplicity—especially when money is involved—is not just appreciated, it's expected.

Getting billing right is no longer optional. It's a competitive edge.

CUSTOMERS SHOULD NEVER HAVE TO CHASE THEIR OWN MONEY

A missed refund. An unexplained charge. A hidden fee. These aren't just clerical errors—they're moments that define how your customer sees you. And if those moments feel dishonest, unfair, or dismissive, no amount of marketing will undo the damage.

In an era of high customer expectations and low switching costs, the billing experience has become a frontline battlefield for trust. And yet too many companies still treat it like a back-office task.

Customers shouldn't have to screenshot transactions, open tickets, or make four phone calls just to get back what's theirs. They shouldn't have to translate legalese to understand what they'll be charged for. They shouldn't have to cancel twice to make sure it actually sticks.

The brands that lead today are the ones who recognize that billing is a moment of service—not just a step in a revenue pipeline. They put customers in control, make charges clear, resolve issues quickly, and most importantly—they act like trust is something they're always earning.

Billing clarity, accuracy, and transparency are no longer differentiators—they're expectations. Fail to meet them, and you won't just lose revenue. You'll lose your reputation.

It's time for leaders to walk the entire billing journey themselves. To feel what it's like to be overcharged. To see what happens when a refund is denied. To understand how quickly confidence is lost when a system fails to serve the very people funding it.

Customers are no longer quiet about their frustrations. They don't just complain. They influence. And when they feel robbed, they don't just leave—they take others with them.

MAKE BILLING WORK. MAKE IT SIMPLE. MAKE IT FAIR.

Mishandling money is a fast way to lose trust. But promising more than you can deliver? That's how you lose credibility at scale.

Key Takeaways

1. Mishandling Money Breaks Trust Faster Than Almost Anything Else

When a company charges quickly but refunds slowly, customers don't see a delay—they see disrespect. Every day they wait feels like a signal that their money, time, and dignity matter less than your process.

2. Billing Is Not Back Office—It's a Moment of Truth

Refunds, disputes, and unexpected charges are not financial issues. They're emotional flashpoints. And when no one owns the outcome, the customer doesn't just feel ignored—they feel defrauded.

3. The Fastest Way to Earn Loyalty Is to Fix a Billing Problem Before the Customer Has to Ask Twice

Trust isn't built through apology emails. It's built through fast resolution, empowered agents, and systems that treat financial clarity as part of the product—not a favor.

CHAPTER 6

Overpromising and Underdelivering

IT STARTED WITH A VIRAL POST.

A lifestyle influencer with over a million followers promoted a new skin-care line on Instagram—clean, sustainable, "luxury without the markup." The videos? Polished. The endorsements? Everywhere. Within forty-eight hours, the product was sold out, with customers gushing about the brand's aesthetic, values, and promise of transformation.

THEN CAME THE DELIVERIES.

Some customers received late shipments. Others opened their long-awaited packages to find leaky containers, generic packaging, or products that didn't match what was advertised. A few didn't receive anything at all.

The company's customer service page flooded with complaints—slow replies, generic responses, and no resolution. Refunds lagged. Apologies were templated. The influencer remained silent.

Soon, social media turned. First a few disappointed comments. Then full exposés. Customers who once celebrated the brand's mission began warning others: "Looks good online. Total letdown."

The disconnect wasn't just about a faulty shipment. It was about a brand that sold an experience and delivered an excuse.

When the Brand doesn't live up to the hype, it raises expectations—and when reality doesn't measure up, the fall is fast, steep, and loud.

When the traveler tweeted their frustration—tagging the brand and referencing the marketing—it went viral. Thousands of others chimed in: "Same here." "Overhyped." "Never again."

The disconnect wasn't just a disappointment. It was betrayal.

That's the power of overpromising. It raises expectations—and when reality doesn't measure up, the fall is fast, steep, and loud.

This chapter unpacks how companies overpromise and underdeliver—intentionally or not—and why the gap between what's sold and what's experienced is one of the fastest ways to destroy brand trust. It's not just a marketing issue. It's a leadership problem.

Because when your brand voice speaks louder than your operational reality, you're not creating excitement—you're setting a trap.

In the pages ahead, we'll explore the root causes of this misalignment, the industries that get it wrong most often, and what the best brands do to deliver on their promises—every time.

THE TRUST EROSION OF OVERPROMISING

At the heart of every overpromise is a broken expectation—and nothing damages trust faster. Customers today aren't naive. They know marketing is polished. But what they won't tolerate is being misled.

The more a brand promises, the more scrutiny it invites. Bold claims—"frictionless onboarding," "AI-powered personalization," "five-star service, every time"—set a high bar. And if the product or experience doesn't match, the backlash isn't subtle. It's swift, public, and enduring.

According to Edelman's Trust Barometer, 67 percent of consumers say they are more likely to stop doing business with a brand if they feel it exaggerated its claims. And a 2023 McKinsey study found that customers who feel "overpromised and underdelivered" are three times more likely to leave than those who experienced a standard service failure.

Why? Because disappointment born of hype feels intentional. It's not seen as a slip—it's seen as manipulation.

This erosion doesn't always come in dramatic waves. It often happens silently—and swiftly. A single broken promise can undo months of goodwill. A customer sees the hype, takes the leap, and is met with disappointment. They don't wait around to file a complaint or request a fix. They just vanish.

And because these losses don't generate support tickets or public backlash, they're often invisible to the business. The customer churns without warning. The marketing team keeps pushing campaigns. Leadership assumes things are working—because no one is tracking the trust erosion happening just beneath the surface.

And in today's fast-moving, hyperconnected marketplace, those losses happen faster than ever. Consumer expectations evolve in real time, driven by digital-first brands that raise the bar with every interaction. If leaders aren't paying attention—if they're not actively walking the experience, listening to feedback, or auditing the message-to-delivery gap—they'll fall behind without realizing it.

Speed matters. And prevention matters even more. Because once the erosion begins, recovery isn't just costly—it's often too late. No complaint. No feedback. Just gone. These are the hardest losses to diagnose—and the most expensive to recover.

Trust lost through overpromising isn't easily rebuilt. Because the next time the brand speaks, customers lean in with skepticism, not anticipation.

Overpromising isn't a growth strategy. It's a trust withdrawal.

To lead in today's market, brands must align their message with their reality. Not just in words, but in execution.

Because the gap between what you say and what you deliver? That's where trust dies.

THE EXPERIENCE GAP (WHAT WAS PROMISED VS. WHAT WAS DELIVERED)

Customers don't buy taglines—they buy outcomes. They don't share your brand promise—they share what actually happened. And when the difference between what was sold and what was delivered is too wide, disappointment turns into distrust.

This is the experience gap—the space between customer expectation and operational execution. It's where inflated messaging collides with incomplete delivery. It's where friction hides, where support teams scramble, and where reputation erodes.

In a 2023 PwC Customer Loyalty report, 59 percent of consumers said they've stopped buying from a brand because "the experience didn't match the promise." The most common offenders? Overhyped tech platforms, luxury service brands, and fast-growing startups that prioritize scale over stability.

The danger of this gap lies in its subtlety. It doesn't always show up as a major failure—it might be the missing follow-up after a big onboarding commitment, or the call that was promised and never made. It might be the service tier that includes "priority access," only for the customer to be placed on hold like everyone else. These moments may seem minor, but in the mind of the customer, they represent a larger truth: This brand says one thing and does another.

The gap widens in companies where marketing and operations don't speak the same language. Where the customer journey map is impressive on paper, but not supported in practice. Where brand teams promise "seamless experiences," but the product requires customers to bridge the gaps themselves.

Consider the software startup that promises "a ten-minute onboarding experience." When implementation takes three calls, two weeks, and a thirty-page PDF, the customer doesn't just feel misled—they feel deceived.

Or the hotel chain advertising "premium oceanfront views," only to check in to a room with a sliver of water over a parking lot.

These aren't just service failures—they're credibility failures. The experience didn't just fall short. It fell through.

And the damage? It's not just one lost customer. It's every potential customer they influence. Because when expectations collapse, customers don't go quietly. They share, post, warn, and amplify.

Bridging the experience gap starts with alignment. Your marketing team, product team, operations, and CX must be connected—not just on goals, but on promises. If your product can't deliver it, your brand shouldn't say it.

Overpromising is easy. Delivering is hard. But sustainable growth only happens when the two are in sync.

Because customers remember the promise. But they never forget what actually happened.

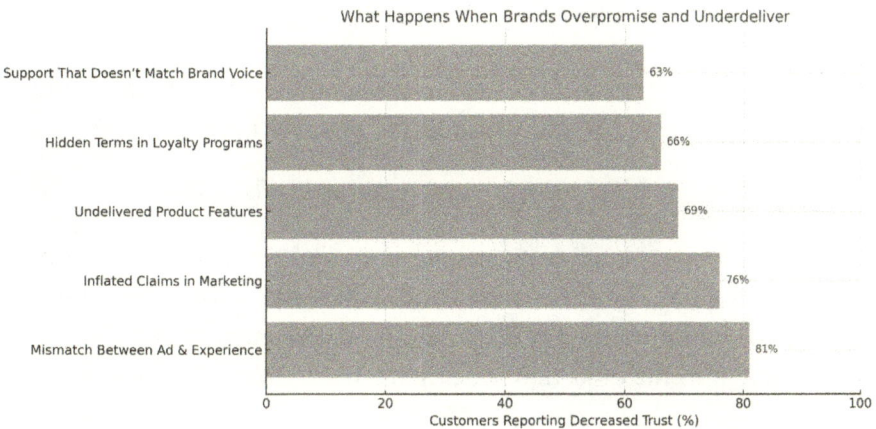

What Happens When Brands Overpromise and Underdeliver

Category	Customers Reporting Decreased Trust (%)
Support That Doesn't Match Brand Voice	63%
Hidden Terms in Loyalty Programs	66%
Undelivered Product Features	69%
Inflated Claims in Marketing	76%
Mismatch Between Ad & Experience	81%

Source: Edelman Trust Barometer 2023; McKinsey Loyalty Trends; Deloitte CX Study 2023.

WHY MARKETING AND PRODUCT
ARE OFTEN MISALIGNED

Most breakdowns between promise and delivery don't come from bad intentions. They come from silos.

Marketing and product teams are often chasing different metrics, speaking different languages, and working on different timelines. Marketing wants to generate buzz and drive acquisition. Product wants to meet deadlines and manage complexity. But beyond priorities, these teams are also incentivized differently. Marketing may be measured on campaign performance, impressions, or lead conversions—while product is judged on delivery speed, stability, and feature velocity. One team is focused on promise and the other on execution.

Too often, these departments compete for budget, executive attention, or organizational influence. Transparency becomes optional. Collaboration becomes sporadic. In many organizations, marketing launches bold messaging without ever checking with product or CX to confirm operational readiness. And product teams, concerned with their own timelines and technical constraints, are rarely looped into what customers are being told to expect.

Without alignment, both sides operate with partial truths. And customers end up navigating the fallout of a promise that was never fully vetted.

That's how the gap is born—and how trust begins to crack.

When marketing teams build campaigns in isolation, they rely on best-case scenarios or early product mockups that may never reflect the real experience. And product teams, buried in development cycles, often have no visibility into the bold claims being made to prospective customers.

That misalignment is compounded in high-growth environments, where speed is prioritized over calibration. The brand promises "seamless onboarding," while the product team knows it's still in beta. The home page features "twenty-four seven white-glove support," while customer service is struggling to staff evenings. These aren't lies—they're gaps in coordination. But to the customer, it all feels the same: You said one thing, and you delivered another.

This disconnect is particularly dangerous in industries like tech, health-care, and hospitality—where emotional stakes are high and customer expectations are nonnegotiable. A missed expectation isn't just a letdown. It's a breach.

The fix starts with shared accountability. Marketing can't operate on aspirational messaging alone. And product can't stay buried in techni-cal deliverables. Both must be held accountable for the promises being made—and the experiences being delivered.

Because a well-orchestrated brand isn't one that dazzles with bold claims. It's one where the story and the experience line up, moment for moment, click for click.

That only happens when marketing, product, and CX stop operating in parallel—and start building the promise together.

WHEN LANGUAGE BECOMES LIABILITY

Words carry weight—especially when they're plastered across ads, land-ing pages, investor decks, and sales collateral. But when those words aren't backed by real-world delivery, they don't just lose credibility—they become a liability.

Language like "frictionless," "effortless," or "game-changing" sounds compelling until it meets a customer's actual experience. If the product requires complex setup, long support times, or inconsistent outcomes, those bold promises can quickly be recast as lies.

In regulated industries, the cost of exaggerated claims goes beyond customer dissatisfaction—it risks legal action. Misleading language in financial services or healthcare isn't just a branding issue; it's a compliance nightmare. But even in nonregulated spaces, exaggerated claims can draw regulatory scrutiny. In 2023, the Federal Trade Commission issued more than seven hundred notices to brands accused of deceptive marketing, citing inflated language and unsubstantiated claims.

In consumer perception, brand language sets the standard by which reality is measured. When there's a gap, the words themselves become evidence of bad intent. "If you said it and didn't do it," the thinking goes, "you meant to deceive me."

Language should inspire confidence—but never overpromise. Great brands ground their copy in what they know they can consistently deliver. They train their teams to write with aspiration, yes, but also with accountability.

Because when customers feel burned, they don't just question the product—they question every word your brand has ever said.

And in a world where feedback spreads in seconds, language doesn't just live on landing pages—it circulates across TikTok rants, Instagram stories, and YouTube exposés. Customers amplify every gap between promise and delivery. Influencers dissect the claims. Reviews get aggregated and reshared. The louder the language, the louder the scrutiny.

That's why messaging alignment can't stop at the marketing department. It has to be shared across the organization. Frontline associates—whether in customer service, retail, or technical support—must understand what the brand is promising and what the product actually delivers. They are the translators of your brand in the real world. When they aren't informed, they fumble interactions, contradict messaging, and compound customer confusion.

Great brands ensure that the front line is trained with the same clarity, discipline, and urgency as the marketing team. Product information needs to be up-to-date, accessible, and honest. Associates need talking points, not scripts. Context, not bullet points. Because the language a customer hears at the last mile matters just as much as the tagline they saw at the top of the funnel.

Overpromising doesn't just start with the wrong message—it spreads when the right people don't have the right knowledge to deliver the experience. That's when language becomes liability in the truest sense.

And perhaps the most corrosive form of that liability is internal. It's when employees know the language is inflated. When frontline teams whisper to each other, "We can't actually deliver that." When the service rep quietly braces for the customer backlash that always follows a misleading ad.

That quiet dissonance erodes internal culture as much as it erodes external trust. Employees lose confidence in the brand they represent. They become reluctant ambassadors—checking boxes instead of championing the mission. And when the people delivering your product don't believe in the promise, it's only a matter of time before customers stop believing it too.

Brands that endure aren't just believable to customers—they're credible to their teams. And that credibility starts with honesty in the message and alignment in the delivery.

BROKEN PROMISES AT SCALE—THE COST OF DISAPPOINTMENT

When a single overpromise backfires, it can hurt. But when that overpromise is baked into every ad, sales call, and social post—across dozens of channels and thousands of touchpoints—the damage multiplies.

This is what happens when brands scale broken promises. And it's one of the most expensive forms of failure.

Because when the message is amplified, so is the expectation. And when operations can't keep up, the gap between words and reality becomes public, loud, and difficult to recover from.

Look at any high-growth startup that over-indexed on marketing before solidifying product. Look at retail chains that scaled too fast without replicating service quality. Or streaming platforms that advertise "limitless content," only to deliver recycled shows. These brands invite disappointment at scale. And they pay for it in returns, complaints, churn, and—most significantly—lost advocacy.

Customers are no longer just buyers. They're broadcasters. And when they feel let down, they don't just quietly opt out. They share, document, and influence others not to make the same mistake.

Worse, internal teams suffer. The support team drowns in escalations. The CX team has to fix what the brand never should've promised. Morale drops. Attrition rises.

According to Accenture, brands that consistently fail to deliver on marketing promises experience a 28 percent higher churn rate and significantly lower lifetime customer value. It's not just the missed transaction—it's the loss of trust that follows.

Disappointment is expensive. And at scale, it's devastating.

That's why the most respected brands aren't just built on storytelling—they're built on operational truth. They ensure that what they promise can be delivered at volume, consistently, and without compromise.

Because keeping your promise once is nice. Keeping it ten thousand times is what makes you a brand worth believing in.

Some of the most admired companies today are operationally honest—brands like Costco, Chick-fil-A, and Patagonia. These companies are known not just for their products but for how reliably and consistently they deliver them. Costco, for example, rarely engages in splashy promotions. Instead, it offers simple value, clear return policies, and a reputation for delivering exactly what it says it will. Chick-fil-A promises fast, friendly service—and its locations are engineered, staffed, and managed to deliver on that promise even during peak hours. Patagonia doesn't just market sustainability—it builds its operations around it, with transparent supply chains and generous return policies that reinforce its message.

These brands don't need to rely on exaggerated claims because their operations do the talking. Their frontline employees believe in what they're delivering. Their systems are designed to meet customer expectations. And their leadership teams understand that sustainable growth comes not from saying more—but from doing better.

Operational truth isn't glamorous. It doesn't generate clicks the way a viral campaign might. But it builds something more valuable: trust that scales. That's the real currency of modern brand loyalty.

CX AND C-SUITE ALIGNMENT FAILURES

The breakdown between what's promised and what's delivered often stems from a deeper disconnect: misalignment between the customer experience function and the executive suite. While the brand pushes bold messages and product hustles to deliver, CX leaders are left in the middle—advocating for the customer, reacting to the fallout, and fighting for visibility.

Too often, CX reports into departments with competing priorities—like marketing, operations, or even finance—where their voice becomes muffled by budget cycles and campaign targets. When the CX function isn't directly connected to strategic decision-making, warning signs get missed. Complaints pile up, sentiment shifts, churn increases—but without a seat at the leadership table, those signals are rarely translated into change.

Meanwhile, the C-suite may be operating with an overly optimistic view of how the brand is performing. Dashboards show top-line growth. Engagement metrics look strong. But what those dashboards often miss are the unvoiced frustrations, the broken trust moments, and the subtle erosion of loyalty playing out daily at the front line.

When executives aren't immersed in the lived customer experience, they lose perspective. They stop walking the property. They start relying on aggregated views and sanitized summaries. And that's when misalignment becomes institutional.

The fix? CX must be elevated to a strategic function—with direct access to the C-suite and a clear mandate to challenge, influence, and lead.

But the internal cultural shift goes deeper than reporting lines. In many companies, customer experience and service teams are still viewed as entry-level roles—teams that "just answer the phones" or "deal with complaints." They're seen as reactive, not strategic. As cost centers, not growth enablers. And as a result, they're rarely included in product discussions, marketing reviews, or executive decision-making until something breaks and noise levels rise.

That mindset is not just outdated—it's dangerous. These are the teams who touch the customer at every friction point. They see where the journey breaks down. They know the patterns in complaints, the confusion in policy, and the frustration that marketing never hears. Ignoring their voice is like driving blindfolded.

Frontline employees aren't just resolving issues—they're absorbing the consequences of broken promises. They're the canaries in the coal mine, the early warning system. When they're left out of the loop or treated as disposable, the organization loses its most direct connection to the truth of the customer experience.

Executives must stop asking, "What are our scores?" and start asking, "What's breaking trust?" They must move from reporting on satisfaction to being accountable for it.

Because when customer experience is treated as a department, it's easy to overlook. But when it's treated as the core of the business, it becomes the standard by which everything else is measured.

COMPANIES THAT DELIVER ON THEIR WORD

Some companies get this right—not by overhauling their messaging, but by aligning their promise with their ability to deliver at scale. These brands build credibility not through clever copywriting, but through consistent execution. They deliver trust, not just marketing.

Take Costco. Their brand promise is simple: Quality goods at fair prices with a no-questions-asked return policy. They don't rely on flashy ads or exaggerated claims. Instead, they earn loyalty by consistently delivering value, both in-store and online. Their CX team reports directly into the operational chain of command, not buried under layers of marketing or finance. That structure ensures issues are addressed, not deflected—and the people closest to the customer have a voice at the table.

Or consider Chick-fil-A, which regularly ranks at the top of customer satisfaction surveys. Their brand promise—fast, friendly, courteous service—is backed by rigorous training, a values-driven culture, and operational discipline. CX is not a cost center there. It's embedded into the DNA of how they serve, staffed and budgeted to be an extension of their brand promise.

Patagonia, widely regarded as a gold standard for brand integrity, builds sustainability not just into its products but into every layer of its customer engagement. Their CX teams are well-informed, empowered, and part of the strategic leadership cycle. They're not there to clean up messes— they're there to uphold the brand's credibility.

And in the tech world, Apple has structured their customer experience teams to partner directly with product, engineering, and retail. Apple's Genius Bar isn't just a support function—it's a feedback loop that helps inform future product design, messaging clarity, and real-time operational fixes.

These companies share three characteristics:

- They give customer experience teams a seat at the table. CX doesn't report to whoever shouts the loudest—it has strategic influence.
- They train their frontline teams in alignment with brand promise. Messaging isn't left to chance. It's shared, operationalized, and enforced.
- They treat CX as a brand driver, not a backstop. Issues are addressed before they escalate. Promises are vetted before they're published.

These brands aren't flawless. But when they make mistakes, they own them—and they recover trust faster than companies who never built that foundation in the first place.

There's also a measurable upside. According to a 2023 McKinsey report, companies that integrate CX into their executive strategy see a 15 to 20 percent increase in customer retention and a 10-plus percent lift in customer lifetime value. When CX is positioned at the heart of decision-making—as it is at Costco, Apple, and Patagonia—teams build with the end experience in mind. They're not guessing at what customers want—they're hearing it directly and baking it into every product launch, service upgrade, and message.

At Apple, for example, the Genius Bar isn't just a retail function—it's a goldmine of feedback. That input is routed back to product and engineering in real time. As a result, fixes are faster, roadmaps are smarter, and the next generation of products is already informed by the friction of the last. That feedback loop drives both loyalty and margin.

In short, brands that elevate CX as a strategic lever don't just build trust—they build resilience. They bounce back faster. They sell more efficiently. And they waste less time fixing what could've been prevented at the start.

THE FIX: GROUNDED MESSAGING, OPERATIONAL READINESS, AND CUSTOMER-FOCUSED TRUTH

Fixing the overpromise problem isn't about pulling back on boldness—it's about earning it. Grounded messaging is about making sure your brand voice reflects not just where you want to go, but where your operations can reliably take the customer today.

That means product, marketing, CX, and operations must come together before anything goes to market. Before a single headline is approved or a new service is promoted, leadership should ask: Can we deliver this—every time, at scale, across markets? If the answer is "not yet," then the message must wait.

Grounded messaging doesn't mean boring. It means being specific, consistent, and deeply familiar with the operational truth on the ground. It means involving the people who talk to customers every day—your support staff, account managers, field teams—in shaping what's promised, because they're the ones who'll be on the receiving end if it's wrong.

Operational readiness is the second pillar. And companies that get it right start by giving their CX and customer service teams a seat early in the development process—not just after a campaign goes live. These teams aren't an afterthought. They're embedded into cross-functional go-to-market planning because they see what customers are asking for, where pain points exist, and what promises will actually land well—or fall flat.

When CX has a voice at the table, product teams hear directly what will work and what won't. When service leaders are in the room during messaging alignment, they can flag potential red flags before they become customer headaches. And when frontline insights shape the plan—not react to it—brands get closer to truth and trust from the start.

Every new campaign should be pressure-tested across frontline teams. Will they have the tools, context, and processes to support the promise? Is the training in place? Is the system load-ready? Are returns and policies aligned?

Brands that succeed here treat readiness like launch criteria—not a post-launch scramble. At companies like Apple, Nike, and American Express, cross-functional go-to-market processes include a CX sign-off, ensuring messaging is grounded in deliverability.

And finally, customer-focused truth. This means communicating clearly, especially when things go wrong. Don't spin delays or service gaps—own them. Customers will forgive imperfections. They won't forgive being misled.

The best brands are storytellers, yes. But they're also truth-tellers. They resist the temptation to oversell and invest in the systems, processes, and people who ensure that what gets promised gets delivered.

Because in the long run, there's no marketing asset more powerful than trust. And trust doesn't come from hype—it comes from honesty, backed by action.

HYPE CAN GET YOU CUSTOMERS— ONLY TRUTH KEEPS THEM

Hype can open doors. It can drive clicks, trial, even virality. But hype without follow-through is a short-term play that damages long-term value. The brands that last are the ones that deliver—again and again—on what they promise.

When you say it, mean it. When you promote it, be ready to support it. When you promise it, be operationally prepared to deliver it at scale.

In a crowded marketplace where customer expectations are rising and patience is shrinking, the only sustainable advantage is truth in execution.

And truth isn't just about honesty in your messaging—it's about operational integrity. It's about backing every word with a system, a process, and a team ready to follow through. Truth-telling becomes truth-doing. It means leadership must not only sign off on the campaign but ensure the company is ready to live it.

That's what earns loyalty.

It's not the clever tagline or the shiny product launch that wins long-term customers—it's the moment a company proves, with clarity and consistency, that what they say is what they do. It's the phone call that gets answered, the return that's processed easily, the feature that works exactly as described.

The smartest brands know that trust isn't built in the tagline. It's built in the moment of interaction when the customer expects something—and actually gets it. That's the promise worth investing in.

Key Takeaways

1. Your Brand Is Not What You Say—It's What the Customer Sees

Customers don't judge your company by your marketing campaigns. They judge it by how your teams act when no one is watching—especially when something goes wrong. If your brand promise is aspirational but your CX is operationally broken, you've created a credibility gap.

2. Every Disconnect Between Story and Experience Is a Loyalty Leak

If your advertising says "frictionless," but your support process requires three logins, or your loyalty program feels like a trap, customers won't call it a mismatch. They'll call it a lie.

3. CX Isn't the Cleanup Crew—It Should Be the Compass

If customer experience teams are only brought in after a product, policy, or campaign launches, then the brand isn't being led by its values—it's being propped up by apologies. Brands that keep promises start by making sure those promises are operationally possible.

CHAPTER 7

You Designed This for You, Not for Me!

Alyssa had made up her mind. After months of paying for a gym membership she wasn't using, she finally opened her laptop, determined to cancel it. She logged into the company's sleek portal, expecting a few clicks and a confirmation email. Instead, she was met with a maze.

The "cancel membership" option was buried three layers deep in submenus. When she finally clicked it, a pop-up appeared:

"To cancel, please chat with our virtual assistant."

A small window slid open. "Hi! I'm FitBot. How can I help you today?" Alyssa typed: I want to cancel my membership.

FitBot responded cheerfully: Great! Are you looking to upgrade, freeze, or change locations?

She replied: No. I want to cancel.

FitBot offered her a link to "explore other membership options."

Five responses later, she typed "CANCEL" in all caps, hoping to trigger a different workflow. FitBot apologized, said it didn't understand, and offered to connect her to an agent. Relief. Except the handoff failed. A message popped up:

"All agents are currently offline. Please try again during business hours."

She tried calling. The phone tree had six options, none of which led directly to cancellation. When she finally reached a representative, she was told she needed her twelve-digit contract ID from her original sign-up email—sent over two years ago. Without it, the rep couldn't proceed "for security reasons." Alyssa asked if they could look it up using her name or email. The answer was no.

The next day, she tried again. This time the chatbot wouldn't connect her to an agent at all. It just kept recycling options. She clicked "speak to a human"—nothing. Just a loop of "I can help you with that!" followed by irrelevant questions. She felt like she was shouting into the void.

After several failed attempts over the course of two months, Alyssa contacted her bank to stop future charges. But the company claimed she hadn't followed the "official cancellation process." They kept billing her.

She tweeted about it. She left a review. She told everyone who would listen: Do not give this company your business. Not because of the product—but because of the process.

That gym didn't just lose Alyssa as a customer—they lost her trust, her future business, and every referral she might have made. All because their process worked exactly as designed: not to serve the customer, but to wear them down.

And here's the truth most companies won't admit: This isn't a bug. It's a business model. One that might reduce churn on paper but increases rage, attrition, and public backlash in practice.

Broken processes don't always show up as outages. Sometimes they show up as policy. As chat scripts. As endless loops dressed up as "efficiency." And they are killing your customer experience.

WHEN THE PROCESS ITSELF BECOMES THE PROBLEM

For most organizations, broken processes don't trigger alarm bells. They aren't as visible as outages. They don't spark an immediate PR crisis. They don't always show up in your NPS dashboard the same way a bad frontline interaction does. But make no mistake: They are draining your business—slowly, silently, and at scale.

Let's be clear: Process is the infrastructure of experience. It's the plumbing behind every moment. And when that infrastructure is leaky, clogged, or confusing, the experience collapses.

Every time a customer has to jump through unnecessary hoops—reenter their information, follow up multiple times, get bounced between departments—you're not just wasting their time. You're telling them that your internal operations matter more than their outcome.

Deloitte research shows that 61 percent of customers have switched brands due to "inconvenient processes or unclear policies." That's not product failure. That's procedural failure.

And these aren't isolated moments. Process failures manifest in every stage of the customer journey:

- A refund that takes twenty-one days instead of three
- A self-service portal that redirects you to a phone line
- A password reset that fails due to a legacy security protocol
- An onboarding workflow that demands paper forms in a digital business
- A policy change that isn't communicated—or worse, that contradicts what the agent says

These aren't edge cases. These are everyday experiences.

HIDDEN COSTS, VISIBLE DAMAGE

What does it cost to run a bad process? More than you think.

According to McKinsey, organizations with fragmented, outdated, or poorly managed processes experience 30 to 50 percent higher operational costs than those that design for simplicity and flow. That includes unnecessary manual work, rework due to errors, higher call volumes, and extended time to resolution.

And it's not just internal cost. It's the reputational cost—the brand damage.

When processes fail, customers don't blame the workflow. They blame you. The brand. The logo on the screen. The leadership team they've never met. And they share their frustration publicly—on review sites, on social media, and most powerfully, in conversations with others.

Salesforce's "State of the Connected Customer" report found that 78 percent of customers will abandon a brand after multiple poor experiences—and 66 percent will do so after just one. Those "poor experiences" often trace directly back to poorly designed or broken processes.

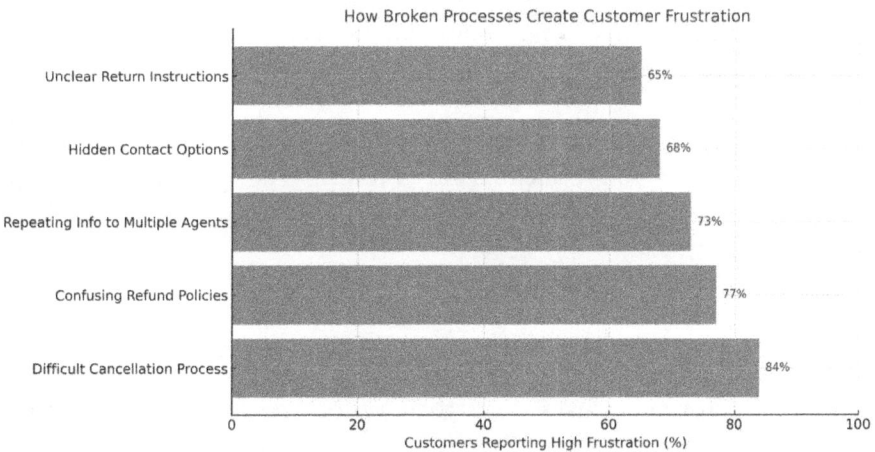

How Broken Processes Create Customer Frustration

Friction Point	Customers Reporting High Frustration (%)
Unclear Return Instructions	65%
Hidden Contact Options	68%
Repeating Info to Multiple Agents	73%
Confusing Refund Policies	77%
Difficult Cancellation Process	84%

Source: Deloitte Digital 2023 CX Trends; McKinsey 'Customer Friction Points' Report; Forrester 2023 CX Index.

THE LOYALTY TAX

Broken processes also punish your best customers. The longer someone does business with you, the more likely they are to need support, manage multiple products, or interact with your systems across channels.

If your process friction gets worse—not better—as customer tenure increases, you're penalizing loyalty.

Worse, when those loyal customers hit a roadblock, they often receive scripted apologies and vague explanations like, "It's just our policy," or "That's how the system works." That's not just frustrating—it's insulting. Especially when the customer knows they've given you their time, trust, and money over the years.

These customers don't just walk away. They walk away angry. And they take others with them.

WHY CUSTOMERS FEEL BETRAYED BY "THE PROCESS"

When customers have a bad experience, they're not always angry because something went wrong. They're angry because they did everything right—and it still didn't work.

They followed the steps. They clicked the links. They waited on hold. They stayed within your policies. And in return? They got stuck in a loop, denied a resolution, or told to start over.

This is where the real damage happens.

The process becomes the villain.

And for the customer, that's worse than a rude agent or a buggy website. Because now, the betrayal feels systemic. Not only did the system fail them—it feels like it was built to fail them.

PROCESS FAILURE IS PERSONAL

Customers don't think in silos. They don't separate billing from support. They don't distinguish marketing from operations. They just know that your process failed them.

- When a return window closes one day before the system allows the label to be printed...
- When a loyalty program update resets their status without warning...
- When an account can't be closed unless a physical letter is mailed...

They don't see policy. They see obstruction. They don't hear logic. They hear, "We don't want to make this easy."

It doesn't matter that these hurdles were intended to prevent fraud, reduce churn, or streamline operations. What matters is that the customer experience was sacrificed—intentionally or not—for internal convenience.

And that's where the betrayal cuts deepest.

THE BUSINESS-FIRST BIAS

Here's the uncomfortable truth: Most business processes weren't designed with the customer in mind. They were designed with the business in mind. They reflect legal risk, operational overhead, revenue leakage, compliance exposure. In other words—they're built to protect the bottom line.

And in doing so, they often alienate the very people funding that bottom line.

What began as a well-intentioned safeguard becomes an instrument of friction. What was meant to minimize loss ends up maximizing attrition.

You see this everywhere:

- Returns processes that create hoops to discourage refunds
- Cancellation flows that require multiple steps or timed holds to deter churn
- Charge dispute policies that burden the customer with documentation, delays, and form fatigue

Companies justify these as risk mitigation. But to the customer, they're the equivalent of being frisked on the way out of a store—it doesn't matter if it's policy. It feels like punishment.

And the psychological impact is worse when the brand's front end told a different story—"fast," "easy," "customer first." The bait-and-switch from brand promise to back-end bureaucracy isn't just frustrating. It's infuriating.

THE COST OF PLAYING DEFENSE

When a company designs its processes around defense, it treats every customer like a potential threat—not a partner. Every safeguard assumes the worst: that you'll lie, cheat, churn, or exploit a loophole.

And while this approach might capture a few bad actors, it alienates thousands of good ones.

- You block a small percentage of fraudulent returns—and lose loyal customers in the process.
- You extend cancellation timelines to salvage revenue—and destroy your NPS.
- You automate resolution to cut labor costs—and drive call volumes higher due to unresolved issues.

Deloitte found that customers are four times more likely to leave a service provider over poor process experience than price. That's not a pricing problem. That's a trust problem. One that starts—and ends—with the processes you chose to build.

THE UNSPOKEN MESSAGE: "WE DON'T TRUST YOU"

Poor processes don't just frustrate—they offend. They send a quiet but unmistakable signal: We don't trust our customers, so we've built walls to protect ourselves from them.

That's how it feels when someone is required to:

- Provide proof of a cancellation made three months ago
- Upload identification to change an email address
- Wait ten to fifteen business days for a refund after a failed transaction

- Navigate a chatbot five levels deep just to find a phone number

To the company, these steps may feel like "control." To the customer, they scream, "We're more interested in covering our backside than helping you."

This mindset is especially dangerous in industries where switching is easy. In SaaS, travel, retail, fintech—the customer has options. If your process requires a customer to do more work than they think is fair, they'll walk. And they'll warn others not to waste their time.

WHEN PROTECTION BECOMES POISON

It's ironic: The very processes designed to protect the business are often the ones doing the most damage to it. Over time, these barriers don't just erode trust. They increase costs. They drive contact volumes, destroy first-call resolution, generate negative reviews, and inflate employee burnout.

Customers feel betrayed not because something went wrong—but because the process worked as intended. It wasn't designed to make things right. It was designed to make things harder. That is the ultimate insult.

And it's the kind of insult customers remember.

What Process Failures Reveal About the Company

EVERY BROKEN WORKFLOW TELLS A BIGGER STORY

Customers don't need an org chart to understand a company's priorities. They can see it in the process.

If the cancellation flow is hidden, the refund policy confusing, and the support path exhausting—they know. The company doesn't really want to help them.

Process failures are never just about inconvenience. They're symptoms of something deeper: internal disconnection, competing priorities, risk aversion, or just plain indifference. And they tell the customer more about your culture than any ad campaign ever could.

THE EXPERIENCE IS THE PROCESS

There's an old saying in operations: Your process is your product. But in today's experience economy, it's more accurate to say: Your process is your brand.

Customers don't separate your mobile app from your call center. They don't care whether your onboarding flow is owned by ops, legal, or product. They only care if it works.

When it doesn't—when a simple task turns into a gauntlet—customers draw their own conclusions:

- This company is disorganized.
- They care more about themselves than me.
- They don't walk their own experience.
- They built this for internal efficiency, not external simplicity.

And here's the kicker: They're usually right.

Most process breakdowns aren't technical failures. They're leadership failures. They reflect what got prioritized—and what didn't. They reveal where no one walked the property. No one tried to do what the customer has to do. No one asked, "Would this be acceptable if it were me on the other side?"

THE SILENCE BETWEEN THE SILOS

Process pain often emerges from one place: silos. Each team optimizes for its piece of the journey, with no ownership of the whole.

- Legal designs terms for risk.
- Tech designs portals for scalability.
- Operations designs scripts for consistency.
- Finance designs refunds for cash flow protection.
- Compliance designs friction for control.

Individually, these decisions make sense. Collectively, they create chaos.

That's how you end up with customer experiences like:

- A billing portal that doesn't sync with account status
- A support team that can't access order history
- An email that links to an expired FAQ
- A self-service path that still requires human approval

And worst of all: a customer caught in the middle with no one accountable.

As Accenture notes, 61 percent of executives admit their organization's internal complexity directly damages customer experience. That's not a technical gap. That's a leadership blind spot.

CULTURAL CLUES IN CUSTOMER PAIN

Process breakdowns are also cultural signals.

- If it takes five approvals to issue a fifty-dollar credit, you don't trust your people.
- If cancellations require a twenty-minute phone call, you prioritize churn prevention over transparency.
- If policy trumps empathy, you've built a rules-first culture—not a customer-first one.

Customers feel that. They might not articulate it in those words, but they sense it. And they translate that feeling into decisions: stay, escalate, warn others, or leave.

Companies like to say, "We care about the customer." But the customer doesn't measure that by intent. They measure it by outcome. By ease. By clarity. By respect.

If your process makes the customer feel like the enemy, the problem isn't the customer. It's you.

INTERNAL EFFICIENCY ≠ CUSTOMER SIMPLICITY

One of the biggest lies companies tell themselves is this: "We've streamlined the process."

What they mean is they've streamlined it internally. Automated it. Centralized it. Structured it.

But in doing so, they've often made it harder externally. Because internal efficiency rarely maps directly to customer simplicity.

A process that looks elegant on a whiteboard—with its logic trees and approval flows and exception-handling branches—may be a nightmare to navigate in real life. Especially when the customer has to do it alone.

And when that happens, the customer doesn't get mad at the system. They get mad at the brand. They assume this was intentional. That you meant to make it this hard.

They may not be wrong.

THE CX AND C-SUITE LEADERSHIP BREAKDOWN

IF YOU'RE NOT WALKING THE PROCESS, YOU'RE LEADING BLIND

Most C-suite executives don't realize how broken their processes are—not because they don't care, but because they're too far removed. They rely on reports, dashboards, and PowerPoint summaries that distill customer pain into a set of sanitized metrics.

But here's the brutal truth: You can't fix what you refuse to feel. And most customer pain is felt in the process.

Executives walk the product. They walk the financials. But very few walk the process—the exact path their customers are forced to take to buy, cancel, return, get help, or escalate. And that disconnect costs companies millions.

DELEGATED TO DEATH

In too many companies, CX is seen as a function—not a strategy. It's assigned to a team, or worse, buried under marketing or operations. And once it's "owned," leaders assume it's handled.

But process pain isn't always visible on a quarterly dashboard. It lives in the weeds. In the policy wording. In the back-end handoff. In the tone of a chat response. It's not just what the customer experiences—it's what they have to go through.

And when leaders don't experience it themselves, they lose sight of how bad it's become.

Executives who delegate customer experience without inspecting it are playing a dangerous game. As McKinsey notes, companies that embed CX as a leadership discipline—not a department—outperform their peers in both revenue growth and customer retention.

THE OPERATIONAL ILLUSION

The most dangerous phrase in leadership is: "That's working as intended."

That usually means someone built the process to satisfy internal needs—but never tested it from the outside in. What leadership sees as "stable" or "compliant," the customer experiences as cumbersome, cold, and confusing.

Consider:

- A customer who must go through twelve clicks to update payment info
- A rep who needs supervisor approval to waive a fifteen-dollar fee
- A form that errors out unless you enter your address exactly as it appears on file

These issues are rarely escalated to the boardroom. But they should be. Because while they may not be classified as "breakage," they are exactly what drives dissatisfaction, churn, and negative word of mouth.

CX TEAMS KNOW. BUT NO ONE LISTENS.

Here's the thing: Your CX and support teams already know where the pain lives. They've heard the stories. They've logged the complaints. They've escalated the same broken workflow over and over again.

But internally, they're often dismissed as noise—"just agents," "just call center people," "entry-level employees." That's a critical mistake.

Because these are the people who hear, every day, in raw, unfiltered language, exactly what customers hate about your process.

Yet in many organizations, they don't have a seat at the table. They're not consulted during policy design, product changes, or tech upgrades. They're called in after the fallout.

Imagine a hospital ignoring nurses while redesigning its emergency department.

That's how most companies treat their customer-facing teams.

ORG DESIGN IS DESTINY

Where CX sits in the org chart says everything about how seriously the company takes the customer experience. If it's three layers down, buried under marketing, ops, or tech, it's a cost center, not a strategic lever.

But when CX reports directly to the CEO or COO—when it has authority, visibility, and a voice—the game changes. Suddenly, customer impact is part of the conversation from the beginning, not just the cleanup crew at the end.

Companies that elevate CX to a leadership-level role consistently outperform those that don't. According to PwC, brands that prioritize CX as a C-level agenda see up to 16 percent higher customer lifetime value than those who treat it as a service function.

In other words, the way you structure CX is the way you signal its importance.

And if you don't empower someone to own and fix broken processes, you're guaranteeing they'll stay broken.

Who Owns the Process? (And Why No One's Fixing It)

WHEN EVERYONE'S RESPONSIBLE, NO ONE IS ACCOUNTABLE

Here's one of the most common sources of friction in the customer experience: No one owns the process from end to end.

Everyone owns a part of it. But that's exactly the problem.

In most organizations, customer-facing processes span five to ten different teams—product, operations, compliance, tech, legal, finance, marketing. Each group has its own metrics, its own priorities, and its own definition of success.

- Legal wants to reduce exposure.
- Ops wants efficiency.
- Tech wants clean requirements.
- Finance wants cost control.
- Marketing wants conversion.

And somewhere in the middle, the customer just wants a refund. Or to cancel. Or to get a question answered without needing a PhD in your company's back-end logic.

But because no single person or team owns the entire journey, what the customer experiences is a disconnected, conflicting, often maddening sequence of handoffs, blind spots, and dead ends.

THE ILLUSION OF OWNERSHIP

Most companies think they have ownership of their processes. After all, someone built the FAQ page. Someone designed the IVR. Someone wrote the policy.

But that's just the paperwork.

True process ownership means someone is accountable for the entire experience—start to finish—as the customer lives it. That includes:

- How easy it is to start the process
- How clear the steps are

- How many systems the customer has to touch
- How long resolution takes
- And what happens when things go wrong

When no one owns all of that, customer experience becomes a patchwork of internal compromises—optimized for internal clarity, not external simplicity.

And it breaks. Every time.

PROCESS BY COMMITTEE = PAIN BY DESIGN

Most processes evolve through meetings. And the more stakeholders in the room, the more complexity gets baked in—because every department adds its layer of protection.

- Legal says, "We need this clause."
- Tech says, "We need this data point."
- Ops says, "We need this handoff."
- Compliance says, "We need this approval step."
- Finance says, "We need this retention window."

Each addition seems small. Harmless. Reasonable. But they add up. And no one in that meeting is asking: What does this feel like to the customer?

That's how you end up with:

- Four-step logins that fail at the second step
- Return policies that require printed forms and packaging slips
- Cancellation flows that reset the clock with every contact
- "Track my order" systems that don't work on mobile

These aren't edge cases. They're the byproduct of unowned, untested, and unaccountable process design.

EVERYONE PROTECTS THE BUSINESS. WHO PROTECTS THE CUSTOMER?

Ask any leader, and they'll tell you they care about the customer. But look at their decision-making, and you'll see the truth: They care about their domain.

- The security team optimizes for risk avoidance
- The finance team optimizes for revenue protection
- The legal team optimizes for liability management
- The tech team optimizes for system stability

All of that is important. But none of it answers the question: Who is optimizing for the customer?

In most companies, the answer is vague. "Everyone is." Which really means—no one is.

And that's how broken processes survive for years. Because they were designed to serve internal priorities, not customer needs.

THE CUSTOMER PAYS THE PRICE

The worst part? Customers don't know—and don't care—that your company is siloed. They don't care if your policy is owned by legal, or if the delay is due to a tech backlog, or if the self-service portal was outsourced to a third-party vendor.

They just know it doesn't work. And they blame you.

When a process is broken and no one owns it, the customer becomes the cleanup crew.

They're the ones who wait on hold. Who send the follow-up. Who resubmit the form. Who chase their own resolution because your org structure isn't aligned to serve them.

That's not just inefficient. It's brand-damaging.

As Salesforce found, 71 percent of customers say they've stopped doing business with a company because the process was "too difficult." Not because the product failed. Because the process failed.

And fixing it isn't a technology issue. It's an accountability issue. One that starts—and ends—with leadership.

COMPANIES GETTING IT RIGHT

Some companies don't just talk about being customer-centric—they build it into the very architecture of their processes. These are the organizations that understand: The best experience isn't the one with the most features or the flashiest tech. It's the one that just works—with as little effort as possible from the customer.

In a world where complexity has become the default, simplicity is a differentiator. And it doesn't happen by accident. It happens by design.

APPLE: FRICTIONLESS TRADE-INS AND SEAMLESS SERVICE

Apple's trade-in program is a masterclass in removing process friction. A customer can walk into any Apple store with an old device and walk out minutes later with credit applied toward a new one—no forms, no waiting periods, no convoluted back-end approvals.

Online, it's just as smooth. Customers are sent prepaid packaging, receive clear tracking updates, and typically get their credit within days of the return being received. No multiple portals. No resubmitting paperwork. No proof of purchase required. Apple already knows—because they built the process around the customer, not internal silos.

Behind the scenes, there's a complex web of logistics, authentication, and valuation. But the customer never sees it. And that's the point. Apple hides complexity, not capability. As a result, they enjoy some of the highest customer satisfaction and loyalty metrics in the tech industry.

AMAZON: THE RETURN PROCESS AS A GROWTH LEVER

Amazon didn't just streamline returns—they made them a competitive weapon. Customers can return most items without repackaging, without printing anything, and without having to talk to anyone. They can drop them off at a Whole Foods, a UPS Store, or even a Kohl's—often with just a QR code and a two-minute interaction.

And here's what's truly brilliant: Amazon issues many refunds before they even receive the item back. That level of trust—backed by predictive analytics and risk controls—signals to customers that the company values their time more than their transaction history.

The results speak for themselves. According to PwC, 63 percent of consumers say a company's return policy plays a significant role in whether they'll do business with them again. Amazon has built loyalty by making one of the most painful processes in retail feel effortless—even generous.

DELTA AIR LINES: PROACTIVE REBOOKING AS PROCESS REDEMPTION

Few industries deal with more complexity than commercial aviation. Yet when Delta leaned into process design through the customer lens, it paid off.

If a customer's flight is delayed or canceled, Delta often rebooks them proactively before they even reach the gate. Through push notifications, app integration, and dynamic rebooking workflows, customers are offered new itineraries with just a tap—eliminating the frustration of waiting in long customer service lines or calling into overwhelmed agents.

Delta didn't eliminate the disruption. They eliminated the work customers would otherwise have to do to resolve it.

This investment in intelligent, customer-facing process automation has led to Delta ranking consistently at the top of J.D. Power's Customer Satisfaction Study in the airline category—despite facing the same weather, aircraft, and staffing constraints as their competitors.

ZAPPOS: EMPOWERING PEOPLE, NOT JUST PLATFORMS

Zappos has long been celebrated for its customer service culture, but what often gets missed is how process plays a role in enabling that excellence. Their philosophy is simple: If a process gets in the way of helping a customer, change the process.

This shows up in small but powerful ways: Agents are empowered to offer free overnight shipping, process full refunds without approval, and spend as long as needed on a call to solve a customer's issue. There are no rigid call-time quotas. No script rigidity. No arbitrary limits on problem-solving.

The result? A process culture that prioritizes resolution, not regulation— and a brand that continues to earn fanatical customer loyalty despite being part of a massive conglomerate (Amazon).

What all these companies understand is this: Great process isn't invisible because it's small—it's invisible because it's intuitive.

These leaders walk their customer journeys. They test what it feels like to cancel, return, change, escalate. And then they invest in making those moments better—even when no one's looking. Especially when no one's looking.

They treat process not as an internal efficiency engine, but as a frontline experience—one that either reinforces trust or destroys it.

THE FIX: DESIGN FOR HUMANS, NOT DEPARTMENTS

IF YOUR PROCESS REQUIRES A MAP, YOU'RE ALREADY LOSING

Broken processes don't require a better script. They require a better design philosophy.

The best companies don't optimize for internal efficiency at the customer's expense. They reverse it. They design around customer ease—and then align the organization to deliver it. That's not just good CX. That's good business.

If you want to fix the friction, stop asking, "How do we make this work better for us?" and start asking, "How do we make this work better for them?"

Here's how.

- Walk the property. Yourself. Often.

  You can't fix what you don't experience.

  Every senior executive should routinely walk the full customer journey—not the ideal version in a slide deck, but the real one your customers live every day. Buy the product. Try to cancel. Request a refund. Submit a support case. File a complaint. Change your address.

  Experience every click, hold, transfer, and escalation—just like a customer would.

  This exercise reveals what dashboards don't. Where policy meets friction. Where tech meets confusion. Where loyalty meets insult.

  As McKinsey puts it: "Companies that understand and redesign end-to-end journeys increase customer satisfaction by 20 to 30 percent, while reducing cost to serve by up to 25 percent."

  In other words: empathy scales. But only when it starts at the top.

- Diagnose, don't decorate.

  Too many companies put new tech on top of old process. That's decorating dysfunction—not fixing it.

  Before you layer on automation, AI, or self-service portals, ask: Is the underlying process even sound?

  - Are steps redundant?
  - Are policies still relevant?
  - Is this flow designed for the customer, or to route work internally?

    ◦ Are success metrics aligned with customer outcomes, or departmental KPIs?

Don't automate the mess. Remove the mess. Then digitize what remains.

- Establish a process owner—with teeth.

If no one owns the full experience, it will stay broken.

Every high-impact process (cancellation, returns, refunds, escalations, account changes) should have a single, named owner with end-to-end accountability—regardless of how many departments touch it.

That owner must have authority to change cross-functional policies, veto complexity, and align teams around the customer. Otherwise, every process becomes a political compromise. And customers pay the price.

Salesforce research shows that 76 percent of customers expect consistent interactions across departments—yet 54 percent say they still experience fragmentation. The solution is leadership, not lip service.

- Use frontline intelligence as strategy input.

Your contact center agents, field reps, and live chat teams have more process insight than any focus group ever will. But most companies fail to turn that insight into strategy.

You need structured feedback loops that capture:

    ◦ Where customers are getting stuck
    ◦ Which workflows create unnecessary escalations
    ◦ What steps confuse, anger, or exhaust customers
    ◦ What policies make employees say, "I'm sorry, I know this is ridiculous."

This isn't anecdotal noise—it's strategic gold. Treat it that way.

Reward teams not just for handling volume, but for surfacing insights that lead to simplification.

- Build for exceptions first.

Most processes are designed for the 80 percent—the average use case. But it's the exceptions that break trust.

The refund that didn't go through. The canceled service that still billed. The change-of-address that wiped the account.

Build your process to handle the edges. That doesn't mean bending to every scenario. It means anticipating failure points, and designing graceful recovery paths.

Recovery is where loyalty is tested. Fail there, and you don't just lose a customer—you earn a critic.

- Shift from control to enablement.

When a customer needs help, your process should feel like a partnership—not a trial.

Instead of asking:

"How do we prevent loss?"

Ask: "How do we enable resolution?"

That might mean trusting your agents to issue credits without three levels of approval. It might mean accepting more returns to retain more customers. It might mean prioritizing trust over tight policy.

If your default assumption is that customers are trying to game the system, you've already lost the relationship.

- Measure what matters.

If your CX scorecards only measure resolution time and handle time, you're missing the bigger picture.

Add metrics that reflect true process health:

- ○ Effort score: How hard was it to complete the task?
- ○ Self-resolution rate: How often can customers solve issues without contacting support?
- ○ Failure rate by stage: Where are customers dropping off?
- ○ Repeat contact rate: How many are returning because the process didn't work the first time?

What you measure is what you prioritize. And if you don't measure friction, you'll never eliminate it.

Ultimately, fixing broken processes isn't about rewriting policy. It's about rewriting intent.

Do you want to protect the business from customers? Or do you want to empower the customer in ways that protect the business?

Only one of those paths leads to growth.

CUSTOMERS DON'T CARE ABOUT YOUR ORG CHART

THEY CARE IF IT WORKS. PERIOD.

Your customer doesn't know who built the portal. They don't know which team owns the policy. They don't care which department is responsible for the delay.

All they know is this. They needed something.

They followed the process, and it failed them.

That failure—whether it was a refund that never came, a cancellation that didn't cancel, or a five-step login reset that still didn't work—becomes a reflection of your brand, not your back-end operations.

Because from the outside, there is no marketing vs. ops vs. legal. There's just you.

When the experience breaks, they don't say,

"Well, the process was probably built by different stakeholders with conflicting incentives."

They say,

"This company doesn't care."

That's the real risk of broken processes. Not just attrition. Not just increased call volume or agent fatigue. But the erosion of trust—invisible at first, then systemic.

BUREAUCRACY DOESN'T SCALE LOYALTY

For far too long, companies have been designing customer processes as if the customer were the problem. That mindset infects every step:

- The fine print
- The circular chatbot
- The policy written in legalese
- The "confirm your identity" loop
- The multiweek refund timeline

It's not just inefficient. It's insulting.

And in a market where switching is one click away—where reviews drive decisions and reputation spreads in seconds—bureaucracy is a liability.

Complexity doesn't protect you. It repels your customers.

Because at the end of the day, the customer doesn't want to read your playbook. They want a fair shot. A clean path. A company that trusts them enough not to make them beg for resolution.

That's what earns loyalty. That's what gets remembered.

Not the product. Not the perks.

The process—when it's invisible, respectful, and human.

Key Takeaways

1. Customers Shouldn't Have to Be Process Experts to Do Basic Things

If your systems are so complex that customers need to escalate, guess, or Google their way through them, you haven't built a journey—you've built an obstacle course.

2. Process Friction Isn't Just Inconvenient—It's Perceived as Indifference

Every extra step, every dead-end chatbot, every "you're in the wrong department" handoff signals one thing: The company didn't care enough to make it easier. And that's when customers stop trying.

3. Great Companies Don't Just Fix Broken Journeys—They Design Them Around the Customer from the Start

Fixing a painful experience after launch is damage control. Involving CX and operations from the beginning is strategy. Process isn't just a back-end issue—it's the brand in motion.

CHAPTER 8

Complicated Polices and Lack of Transparency

Ryan wasn't trying to game the system. He'd been a loyal customer for over four years—subscribed to the service, paid on time, rarely called support. He knew the cancellation deadline was coming up, so he logged in to his account three days before the end of the billing cycle. The button that said "cancel membership" was grayed out.

Strange, he thought. Maybe a glitch. He opened the help page. Nothing there. He clicked through a few articles, started a chat, and finally got through to a human who told him—cheerfully—that cancellations must be processed five days before the next billing cycle, per Section 4.2 of the Terms and Conditions.

Ryan stared at the message.

Five days?

Where was that disclosed?

Why wasn't it anywhere near the "cancel" button?

Why hadn't anyone mentioned it in the reminder email?

The agent copied and pasted the clause into the chat. "We understand your frustration," they wrote. "But, unfortunately, that's our policy."

Ryan didn't argue. He didn't beg. He just closed the tab. But in that moment, something snapped. He realized this wasn't a glitch. It was a tactic.

The policy hadn't been written to create clarity. It had been written to create control. To turn a deadline into a revenue lock-in. To give the company cover while the customer carried the cost.

It wasn't about the money. It was about the message:

We don't trust you. And we don't expect you to read the rules—until they benefit us.

He'd been a loyal customer for four years. Now? He would never come back.

And he wouldn't keep it to himself.

IT'S IN OUR POLICY AND THE HIDDEN TOLL OF OPAQUE POLICIES

WHEN THE RULES FEEL RIGGED, THE RELATIONSHIP IS ALREADY LOST

Most companies don't set out to deceive their customers. But that's exactly how it feels when the rules aren't visible until after the fact.

Customers encounter a policy not during onboarding, but at the moment of disappointment. The return window has closed. The refund exception doesn't apply. The grace period never existed. The cancellation deadline was "clearly stated"—somewhere buried in a seventeen-page terms document.

These aren't policies. These are ambushes.

And customers don't respond to them with understanding. They respond with a fundamental shift in how they view the brand.

What once felt like an honest relationship now feels transactional. Conditional. Opportunistic.

According to Salesforce's State of the Connected Customer report, 66 percent of customers say they've stopped buying from a company because of a policy that felt unfair—and 58 percent say the policy wasn't clear until it was enforced.

The cost isn't just lost revenue. It's accelerated churn. It's negative word of mouth. It's the feeling that the company wasn't built to serve—it was built to shield itself.

POLICIES AREN'T JUST LEGAL TOOLS. THEY'RE BRAND SIGNALS.

Every policy you publish is a signal. Not just of what customers can and can't do—but of how your company thinks.

Do you expect the customer to memorize timelines and terms?

Do you put the burden on them to interpret complex refund scenarios?

Do you make it easier to sign up than to cancel?

If so, you're not writing policy. You're setting a trap.

And customers know it.

They know when the language is vague on purpose.

They know when support staff are hiding behind the rules.

They know when the policy wasn't written to solve problems—it was written to deflect them.

And once they come to that conclusion, your brand's credibility erodes—fast.

Because no one wants to enter a relationship where the rules only appear when it's too late to do anything about them.

THE EMOTIONAL TOLL: BETRAYAL DISGUISED AS BUSINESS LOGIC

What makes opaque policies so dangerous is that they're emotionally dissonant. They look professional, structured, and logical—but they feel dishonest.

A customer who's just been told they're out of policy doesn't care how legally sound the rule is. They care that it wasn't clearly communicated. They care that it was enforced without flexibility. They care that the company didn't even try to meet them halfway.

This disconnect triggers an emotional response that's disproportionate to the infraction—because it's not about the return or the fee. It's about the realization that the relationship was never built to be fair.

And fairness is the cornerstone of trust.

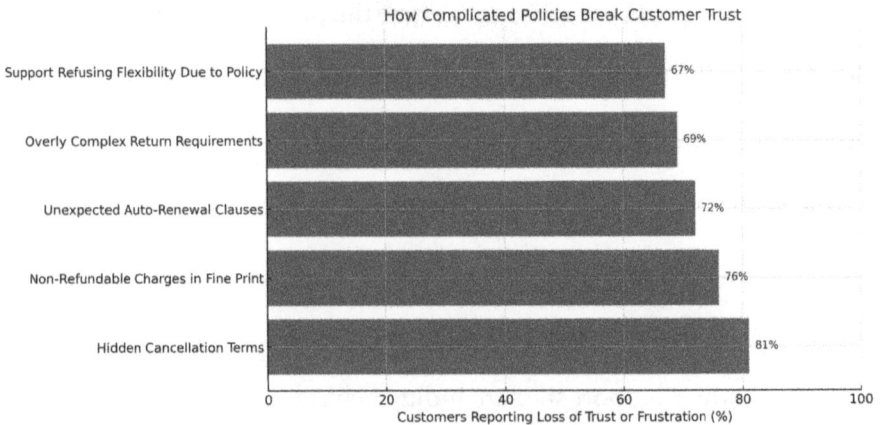

How Complicated Policies Break Customer Trust

Category	Customers Reporting Loss of Trust or Frustration (%)
Support Refusing Flexibility Due to Policy	67%
Overly Complex Return Requirements	69%
Unexpected Auto-Renewal Clauses	72%
Non-Refundable Charges in Fine Print	76%
Hidden Cancellation Terms	81%

Source: Salesforce 2023 State of the Connected Customer; PwC Experience is Everything Study; Forrester Policy Impact Report 2023.

WHY CUSTOMERS FEEL DECEIVED

IT'S NOT JUST THE POLICY—IT'S WHEN YOU ENFORCE IT AND HOW IT MAKES THEM FEEL

Most customers don't wake up looking for a loophole. They don't scour your site to memorize every clause. They assume that if something's important, you'll tell them. If a condition will impact their money, their cancellation, or their access, it will be clear—not buried.

So when they discover a restrictive policy after the moment it mattered—after they clicked, signed, or returned—they don't just feel surprised. They feel set up.

This is the point where customer patience turns into suspicion.

Where disappointment turns into disbelief.

Where they stop assuming good intent.

Because if a company had every chance to be clear—and chose not to be—then the customer can't help but ask: Was this designed to help me fail?

FINE PRINT FEELS LIKE A FINE TRAP

Let's call it what it is: Most "terms and conditions" are written for one purpose—to protect the company. And customers know it.

They know those agreements aren't designed to be read. They're designed to be accepted without scrutiny. The formatting alone—small fonts, long paragraphs, legal language—sends a signal: This is not for you. This is for us.

So when companies hide behind that language in moments of tension, customers don't feel reassured. They feel punished for trusting you in the first place.

According to PwC, 64 percent of customers say they've felt "blindsided" by a policy they weren't aware of—and 48 percent say it made them feel the company was "intentionally misleading."

The intent may not have been deception. But the experience of deception is what matters. Because experience—not legal logic—defines loyalty.

TIMING IS THE TRIGGER

If a refund policy is hard to find, but enforced aggressively?

If a cancellation window is tucked into a footnote, but blocks a full month of charges?

If an exception is denied because of a clause the customer never saw?

That's not a process failure. That's a moment of character—and customers are watching.

They're watching not just what the company does, but when it chooses to act.

They're watching not just what the policy says, but when they hear about it.

They're watching how quickly the company turns from friendly to rigid when money is involved.

And when those shifts happen too fast, too harshly, or too often—the customer stops seeing the brand as a partner. They start seeing it as a predator.

EMPATHY WITHOUT AUTHORITY IS INSULTING

Nothing fuels customer anger more than being told, "We understand," by someone who has no power to do anything about it.

"We're sorry—but that's our policy."

"We hear you—but we can't make an exception."

"We agree it's frustrating—but our hands are tied."

This kind of language doesn't validate the customer. It invalidates their experience. It tells them: "We know you're right—and we still won't help you."

That's not empathy. That's evasion.

And from the customer's perspective, it feels worse than a flat-out denial. Because it means the agent wants to help, but the company has chosen policy over people.

The customer doesn't just feel denied. They feel dismissed. And they're right to ask: If the people talking to customers every day aren't trusted to use judgment, what does that say about the culture?

PERCEPTION IS REALITY—AND PERCEPTION SPREADS

One customer who feels misled can become five. One unfair policy enforcement turns into a Reddit thread. One angry post about a refund denial gets shared, screenshotted, and elevated as proof that this company can't be trusted.

And in that moment, you're not defending your terms. You're defending your intent.

Because in the age of transparency, policy isn't a back-office function. It's a brand signal. It tells the world whether you're in the business of protecting your customers—or protecting yourself from them.

WHAT IT SAYS ABOUT YOU

YOUR POLICIES SPEAK LOUDER THAN YOUR MISSION STATEMENT

Every company says the right things. They talk about customer-centricity, transparency, and trust. But those values aren't measured by what's printed on the wall or posted on a website. They're revealed in the policies your customers encounter—and in how those policies are enforced.

If your refund policy makes people feel like they've done something wrong for asking, that's your brand.

If your cancellation process feels like a maze, that's your brand.

If your terms are crafted to obscure reality rather than clarify it, that's your brand—no matter how polished your marketing.

When a customer hits your policy wall at the exact moment they need fairness, and instead finds rigidity, what they experience isn't structure—it's a strategy. They don't assume the policy was written with good intent.

They assume it was written to protect you, not them. And they're usually right.

They don't walk away thinking, "Well, that's just the rules."

They walk away thinking, "You knew this would happen. And you made it hard on purpose."

POLICIES ARE PRODUCT—NOT PAPERWORK

Inside most companies, policies are owned by legal, risk, or finance. They're drafted in isolation, focused on coverage and compliance. Then they're handed to operations and CX teams to deliver—with little flexibility or frontline discretion.

But what's missed in that process is that policies shape the entire customer experience. They're not back-office documents. They're frontline design.

They influence whether a customer buys, renews, or recommends. They determine if the support team can resolve a tense moment—or make it worse. They show up in reviews, complaints, and social media posts long after the transaction is over.

And when they're not clear, consistent, or compassionate? They become brand liabilities.

Companies that reframe policy as part of the product—something to be tested, improved, and experienced like any other feature—don't just reduce complaints. They build credibility.

A customer who understands the rules, agrees with the fairness, and sees them applied with empathy is far more likely to stay loyal—even when things go wrong.

THE MOMENT YOU SAY, "THAT'S OUR POLICY," YOU'RE NOT DEFENDING. YOU'RE EXPOSING.

The phrase "That's our policy" doesn't resolve anything. It ends the conversation, but it opens the wound.

Customers don't feel reassured by it. They feel dismissed. They hear it as code for "we could help you, but we won't." It tells them they've hit the edge of what your company is willing to do—and that edge, once seen, is never forgotten.

No matter how thoughtful your branding is, how seamless your app is, or how human your social voice may be, the second your policy is used as a shield rather than a tool, it resets the relationship.

REAL CUSTOMER-CENTRICITY ISN'T ABOUT THE EASY MOMENTS

It's not hard to serve customers when everything's going smoothly. The real test comes when they're confused, frustrated, or facing a gray area.

That's when your policies come off the shelf.

That's when your culture shows up.

That's when the customer sees whether the values you promote actually make it into your decisions.

If your teams have no flexibility, if your policies leave no room for context, and if your rules are built to say "no" by default—then your company isn't customer first. It's policy first. And customers can feel the difference.

They may not call it that. But they'll leave. Quietly at first. Then vocally.

And they'll leave not because the answer was no—but because the reason was never human.

THE CX AND C-SUITE LEADERSHIP BREAKDOWN

IF YOU HAVEN'T READ YOUR OWN POLICIES LATELY, YOUR CUSTOMERS ARE ALREADY PAYING FOR IT

Ask a senior executive when they last read their company's cancellation policy—not approved it, but actually read it the way a customer would. Ask them how many steps it takes to file a dispute, or whether their refund window starts from the date of purchase or the date of delivery.

Most won't know. And that's not a judgment—it's a reality. Policies are treated as plumbing: invisible unless something leaks.

But in today's environment, the leaks are everywhere. And they don't just result in complaints—they result in erosion. Erosion of trust. Erosion of perception. Erosion of what customers believe about your company's intentions.

And the truth is, those leaks didn't come from the front line. They were designed upstream.

WHEN POLICY DESIGN HAPPENS IN A VACUUM

In most organizations, policies are created by those who are furthest from the customer: legal teams, risk officers, procurement, or finance. Their job is to protect the business—and they do it well. But they're rarely in the room when the angry emails arrive. They don't hear the sigh on the support call. They don't see the social post that goes viral because a company "followed its policy" and lost a longtime customer in the process.

That disconnect creates policy blind spots. Rules that make sense on paper fall apart in the real world. What's legally sound becomes emotionally tone-deaf.

And yet the default response from leadership is often to double down. Tighten the terms. Train agents to recite them more consistently. Make fewer exceptions—all in the name of efficiency or precedent.

But what it really shows is this: No one is advocating for the customer at the moment policy meets pain.

CX TEAMS ARE TOO OFTEN BROUGHT IN TO ENFORCE—NOT INFLUENCE

Customer experience leaders aren't consulted when the refund language is drafted. They're not asked how customers will interpret a new subscription clause. They're not in the room when policy shifts from flexible to firm.

Instead, they're handed the outcome and told to deliver it with empathy.

This is why so many support teams feel like the face of decisions they never made. They're expected to humanize policies that weren't designed with humans in mind. And they're held accountable for how customers react—without ever having had the authority to shape the policy in the first place.

It's a lose-lose: The customer feels mistreated, and the employee feels powerless.

LEADERSHIP'S REAL RISK ISN'T ABUSE—IT'S ATTRITION

The common justification for rigid policy is protection. We can't afford to set a precedent. We don't want to be taken advantage of. We need consistency across regions.

But the actual risk to your business isn't the one customer who bends the rule. It's the hundreds—or thousands—who see the rule, feel mistreated by it, and decide to take their money elsewhere.

Those customers don't file complaints. They just disappear. Quietly. Permanently. And often with a story they'll share when someone else asks, "Have you ever used that company?"

You may never know how many of them you lost. But you'll feel the attrition. You'll see it in NPS. In retention. In a brand that no longer gets the benefit of the doubt.

POLICY IS CULTURE IN WRITING

If you want to know what your company really believes, don't read the brand manifesto. Read the returns policy. The cancellation process. The "exceptions" section.

If it's hard to understand, hard to find, and hard to navigate—then what you've said to the customer is this: We're here for you. Until it costs us.

Great companies close that gap. They involve CX early. They test policies with real customers before rollout. They empower frontline teams to interpret the rule, not just recite it. And they view exceptions not as risk, but as an opportunity to prove their values under pressure.

Because that's what leadership is. It's not what you approve in theory. It's what you're willing to defend in practice—especially when the rule says no, but fairness says yes.

COMPANIES GETTING IT RIGHT

SIMPLE POLICIES ARE A COMPETITIVE ADVANTAGE—THESE BRANDS KNOW IT

Great customer experience isn't just about friendly people or polished design. It's about creating systems that feel human—especially when things don't go as planned. That includes your policies.

The best brands don't wait for legal to set the tone. They design policies with empathy, enforce them with judgment, and treat exceptions not as liabilities, but as moments to deepen trust.

Here are three companies that have made policy a strategic asset—not just a legal shield.

REI: TRUST WRITTEN INTO THE TERMS

REI, the outdoor gear co-op, has long been known for its generous return policy. But it's not just generous—it's clear, fair, and easy to find.

The company explicitly invites customers to return used gear if it didn't meet expectations. No shaming. No fine-print traps. Just a simple understanding: The gear should work for your adventure—and if it doesn't, they'll make it right.

That clarity isn't accidental. It's built on a business model that trusts its customers—and in turn, customers trust them back. Returns don't spike. Abuse is rare. But loyalty? It's built into the business.

REI understands that a transparent policy is a reflection of brand values. When you trust the customer first, they usually don't make you regret it.

TRADER JOE'S: NO QUESTIONS, NO COMPLEXITY, JUST YES

At Trader Joe's, there's no extensive return process. No manager override. No receipt rigmarole.

You bring something back, say it didn't work for you, and they refund you. Cheerfully. Quickly. Without hesitation.

There's no hidden clause. No "within fourteen days" condition. No policy printed in microscopic font at the bottom of a shelf tag. Just a simple expectation: If you're not happy, we'll fix it.

And customers respond by doing something remarkable—they don't take advantage. They come back. They recommend it. They feel respected. And they reciprocate that respect by being honest.

Trader Joe's proves that generosity scales—when it's paired with trust and consistency.

ALLY BANK: TRANSPARENCY AS PRODUCT DIFFERENTIATION

In financial services—one of the most opaque industries on earth—Ally Bank built its brand around clarity.

Their policies are explained in plain English. Fees are spelled out upfront. Customers aren't left guessing what will happen if they overdraft, transfer, or miss a deadline.

But Ally didn't stop at transparency. They made customer-friendly terms part of the product: no maintenance fees, no surprise penalties, and easy opt-outs. And when something doesn't go right, agents are empowered to resolve it without a "let me check with my manager" runaround.

They made trust operational. Not aspirational.

The result? A brand that feels different—not just because of its voice, but because of its policy posture.

WHAT THESE COMPANIES UNDERSTAND

REI, Trader Joe's, and Ally don't have perfect customers. They don't avoid risk. And they still write policies with clear terms.

But they do something most companies won't: They assume good intent.

They make it easy to understand the rules. Easy to engage. Easy to fix.

And when customers run into an edge case or a gray area, they don't encounter a wall. They encounter a person—empowered to do the right thing.

That's the difference.

Not just between a good experience and a bad one—but between a brand you trust and one you leave.

THE FIX: CLARITY, CONTROL, AND CONTEXT

IF YOU WANT TO BE TRUSTED, STOP HIDING BEHIND THE RULES

Most policies don't break trust because of what they say. They break trust because of how they're written, when they're enforced, and who's allowed to interpret them.

Fixing that requires more than redlining terms and updating web pages. It demands a total shift in how your organization views the role of policy—from risk containment to relationship protection.

That starts with three principles: Clarity, Control, and Context.

CLARITY: IF THE CUSTOMER CAN'T UNDERSTAND IT, THEY CAN'T TRUST IT

Too many policies are written for internal review, not customer reality.

You can't claim transparency and bury critical details three clicks deep. You can't preach empathy and hand your agents scripts that start with "per our terms and conditions." And you can't build loyalty if your policies feel like riddles.

Clarity means writing in plain language. It means putting the most important details up front—not in footnotes. It means designing policy pages with user experience in mind, not legal review order.

Most of all, it means making sure the customer sees the policy before it becomes a problem—not only when it becomes one.

Because if the rule only reveals itself at the moment of conflict, it's not a rule. It's a trap.

CONTROL: LET THE CUSTOMER OPT IN—DON'T TRAP THEM IN

Customers don't just want clear policies. They want agency.

They want to know what they're agreeing to—and they want the ability to walk away if they don't. This means making cancellation, return, and dispute processes as accessible as sign-up. It means removing dark patterns, prechecked boxes, and hidden timelines.

And it means giving customers the ability to say, "No, thanks," without punishment.

Policies that feel inescapable—or designed to delay—aren't just frustrating. They feel predatory.

Giving customers control doesn't just reduce complaints. It increases confidence. Because when people know they can leave easily, they're more likely to stay.

CONTEXT: GIVE YOUR PEOPLE THE POWER TO DO THE RIGHT THING

A good policy provides structure. A great one allows judgment.

Frontline teams should never feel forced to deliver outcomes they know are unfair—just because the rules say so. And customers should never feel like they're being punished for nuance.

That's where context comes in. Empower agents to escalate. Build pathways for exceptions. Track which policies generate the most complaints—and adjust them.

Yes, consistency matters. But so does humanity.

And when you train your teams to understand the spirit of the policy—not just the letter—you build something far more valuable than compliance: credibility.

THIS IS NOT JUST A CX PROJECT—IT'S A LEADERSHIP STANDARD

You don't need thirty new policies. You need 30 percent more transparency, 50 percent fewer legal clauses, and 100 percent more trust that your people can make the call when it matters most.

If your company claims to be customer-obsessed, prove it where it counts—not in slogans, but in terms.

Because policies are a mirror. They reflect what you really believe about your customers.

Make sure they say something worth believing in.

CUSTOMERS DON'T WALK AWAY BECAUSE YOU SAID NO—THEY WALK AWAY BECAUSE IT DIDN'T FEEL FAIR

Policies are necessary. They protect your business. They create structure. They help manage scale. But when policies feel intentionally complicated, inconsistently enforced, or clearly tilted in the company's favor, customers don't see structure. They see strategy. They see defense, not service.

And in that moment, the relationship shifts.

They stop trusting the friendly branding and start remembering how quickly it gave way to cold rules. They stop assuming you'll make it right and start screenshotting every interaction. They stop giving you the benefit of the doubt—and they give it to someone else.

Here's the hard truth: Most customers don't expect perfection. They expect fairness. They're willing to accept boundaries. They're even willing to accept "no." But what they won't accept is the feeling that the rules were written to win against them.

That's not an experience problem. It's a leadership problem.

Because policies don't just govern what happens when things go wrong. They define the experience customers have when they need you most.

You don't need to say yes to everything.

You don't need to approve every refund or exception.

But you do need to build policies that reflect your values—and train your teams to apply them with judgment, not fear.

Because when customers encounter your policy, they're not just reading the rules.

They're reading you.

Key Takeaways

1. Policies Are Brand Signals—Customers Read Them Closely

Every clause, exception, and enforcement choice sends a message about your company's values. When policies feel hidden, rigid, or self-serving, customers assume the worst—and take their loyalty elsewhere.

2. Clarity and Control Build Confidence—Not Just Compliance

Policies written in plain language, presented up front, and designed with customer agency in mind don't just reduce complaints—they increase trust. When people feel in control, they're more likely to stay.

3. Judgment at the Front Line Is Your Culture in Action

A truly customer-centric company doesn't just write better policies—it empowers people to apply them with discretion. Context, flexibility, and fairness aren't soft skills—they're strategic differentiators.

CHAPTER 9

Failure to Resolve the Problem

There's a moment every customer dreads—a moment when an issue arises, and despite years of loyalty, they feel utterly abandoned by the very company they once trusted. Picture this: You've been a loyal customer for years.

You rarely complain, always giving the benefit of the doubt when minor hiccups occur. But today, something significant goes wrong. Perhaps your account is locked without warning, a refund you were promised never materializes, or an expensive service you rely on suddenly stops working. Naturally, you reach out to customer support, expecting a swift and empathetic resolution. Instead, you're met with long wait times, scripted responses, and agents who seem as puzzled as you are.

They offer polite apologies, promise to "look into it," and assure you that someone will follow up—but as days turn into weeks, nothing happens. You call again, repeat your issue for the third time, and are passed along from one department to the next. At this point, it's not merely frustration that overwhelms you—it's a profound sense of invisibility. In that moment, the painful truth dawns: This company doesn't value me.

This is the moment when brand loyalty shatters. When a customer feels that their problem is unimportant, they begin to question the very foundation of the relationship. Instead of feeling cared for, they feel like just another number in an endless queue—a ticket to be processed rather than a valued individual. And once that realization sets in, there's little chance of winning them back.

Like a slow-burning fuse, each unresolved issue chips away at trust until the customer finally reaches their breaking point: They leave, cancel their subscription, demand a refund, and often take to social media or word of mouth to warn others about their terrible experience.

A $19 PROBLEM THAT COST A BRAND A $2,000 CUSTOMER

Her order had arrived—two candles, one broken. A small issue. Easy to resolve. Or so she thought.

She started with the website's help center. After scanning five drop-down menus and a maze of FAQs, she finally found a buried "Contact Us" form. She filled it out, uploaded a photo of the broken candle, and waited.

Three days later, she received an auto-response: "We're sorry for the inconvenience. Please provide more details about your issue so we can assist," she replied, confused. She had already included all the details. Photo. Order number. Description. Still, she answered again.

Two more days passed. A new agent responded, "Please confirm the item number and the condition of the product." It was the third time she'd explained it.

By now, it had been six days, three emails, and no progress. She called the support line. After a fourteen-minute hold, a rep told her they couldn't issue a refund without approval from another department. Samantha asked to speak with that team. "They don't take customer calls," the agent said. "We'll escalate your request and someone will get back to you."

No one did. Two weeks in, she gave up.

The broken candle was worth nineteen dollars. But over the past year, Samantha had spent nearly $2,000 with the brand—as gifts, holiday orders, and corporate thank-you packages.

She didn't yell. She didn't demand anything outrageous. She just wanted someone to take ownership and make it right. Instead, she got the slow drip of indifference:

Generic messages. Multiple handoffs. No accountability.

The problem wasn't that something went wrong.

The problem was that no one acted like it mattered.

THE HIDDEN TOLL OF FAILING TO RESOLVE THE PROBLEM

WHEN RESOLUTION FAILS, THE RELATIONSHIP FAILS WITH IT

When something goes wrong in the customer journey—and it inevitably will—what happens next determines everything.

Most customers don't expect perfection. But they do expect ownership. They expect someone to fix the issue with urgency, empathy, and a sense that their time and loyalty are worth protecting.

Failing to resolve a problem isn't just a service failure. It's a trust failure. And it's often the moment when an otherwise satisfied customer quietly decides: never again.

RESOLUTION ISN'T A PROCESS—IT'S A PROMISE

Too many companies confuse the completion of a ticket with the resolution of a problem. They believe that sending a confirmation email or closing a case means the issue is handled. But from the customer's point of view, the experience hasn't ended until it feels complete, fair, and human.

According to Salesforce, 88 percent of customers say the experience a company provides is as important as its products or services. That includes what happens after something breaks. Especially then. When resolution feels cold, corporate, or robotic, customers don't feel taken care of—they feel like a number. And that's when the emotional break begins.

THE EMOTIONAL COST OF FEELING UNIMPORTANT

Customers rarely remember the original issue as clearly as they remember the way they were treated. The broken product fades. The delayed service gets resolved. But the feeling of being dismissed—of being bounced, brushed off, or ignored—sticks.

- It sticks when they have to retell the story five times.
- It sticks when they get a generic response instead of a solution.
- It sticks when no one takes ownership, and no one follows up.

And once that emotional erosion sets in, it's difficult to reverse.

Gartner research shows that customers who experience high-effort interactions are nine times more likely to churn than those whose problems are resolved with ease. Nine times. That's not a rounding error. That's a loyalty killer. The core issue isn't the problem—it's how the company makes the customer feel while trying to fix it.

THE OPERATIONAL MYTH OF "CASE CLOSED"

Leadership dashboards are often littered with resolution stats: average handle time, time-to-close, number of open tickets. But these numbers can be dangerously misleading.

You can close a ticket without resolving a problem. You can meet your SLA and still lose the customer. You can check the box—and still break the relationship.

Because what happens behind the scenes—the transfers, the apologies, the scripts, the escalations—doesn't show up in the metrics. But it does show up in customer sentiment. In attrition. In the stories people tell their friends.

Accenture reports that 69 percent of customers say they've switched brands because of poor service—and the number one reason cited? Being passed around without a solution. These are not "service issues." They are leadership issues, rooted in how the company defines, designs, and empowers resolution.

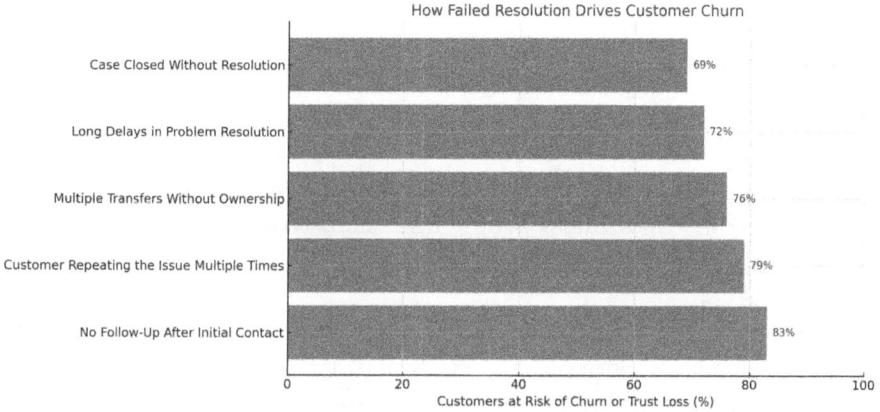

How Failed Resolution Drives Customer Churn

Category	Percentage
Case Closed Without Resolution	69%
Long Delays in Problem Resolution	72%
Multiple Transfers Without Ownership	76%
Customer Repeating the Issue Multiple Times	79%
No Follow-Up After Initial Contact	83%

Customers at Risk of Churn or Trust Loss (%)

Source: Gartner 2023 CX Loyalty Study; Accenture Consumer Pulse; Salesforce Service Benchmark Report 2023.

THE MULTIAGENT RUNAROUND

One of the clearest signs of systemic failure is the repeat explanation loop.

Customers describe it the same way across industries:

"I had to start over every time."

"No one read the notes."

"It felt like no one actually wanted to help—they just wanted me off the phone."

This isn't just inefficient. It's insulting. It signals a complete lack of internal coordination, data continuity, and customer empathy.

And every time a customer has to retell their story, it doesn't just increase their frustration—it devalues the entire brand. You're saying: "Your time isn't valuable enough for us to get this right the first time."

In an age of advanced CRM systems, real-time data, and unified communications, that's not a technology problem. It's a priority problem.

EMPLOYEE COST: THE OTHER HIDDEN CASUALTY

Resolution failure doesn't just impact customers—it demoralizes employees.

Agents know when they're letting customers down. They know when they're enforcing policies that don't make sense, apologizing for systems that don't work, or transferring problems they could fix if they were allowed.

This creates frustration, burnout, and disengagement. Employees who joined the company to help people find themselves trapped in a reactive loop—explaining what they can't do instead of empowered to act on what they should do.

Over time, this corrodes morale. High performers leave. Remaining staff go into autopilot. And the cycle of mediocrity repeats—masked by a thin layer of operational metrics.

WHEN THE FAILURE IS INVISIBLE, THE IMPACT ISN'T

Customers don't always make noise when they're disappointed. They don't all leave angry reviews or flood your inbox. Most just quietly vanish. They churn without a trace. And if you're only measuring success by what you can see—call logs, survey responses, ticket closure rates—you'll miss the churn happening in silence.

And that's the cost most companies never account for:

The customers you didn't even know you lost—because no one resolved what could have been a minor issue, if only someone had acted like it mattered.

THE CX AND C-SUITE LEADERSHIP BREAKDOWN

WHAT LEADERS CALL "LOW PRIORITY" IS OFTEN WHAT CUSTOMERS REMEMBER MOST

In most organizations, senior leaders pride themselves on strategic thinking, investment prioritization, and big-picture alignment. They obsess over growth, brand trust, digital transformation. But ask them to describe what a customer experiences when trying to get a billing error corrected, or a missing package replaced, and you'll get blank stares—or, worse, assumptions.

That's because in the C-suite, resolution doesn't feel urgent. It's viewed as a service function. A queue. A tactical problem that gets addressed "down there." But for the customer, resolution is the moment where all the company's promises are tested. When they reach out, it's not just about fixing a glitch. It's about discovering whether the brand they chose actually respects them.

And this is where the disconnect begins.

THE EXECUTIVE BLIND SPOT

Many senior leaders assume that because they've staffed a support team, implemented a CRM, and put SLAs in place, the problem of resolution is solved. They're handed dashboards full of closure rates, handle times, deflection metrics, and escalations logged. But what those dashboards rarely reveal is how customers felt about the resolution—or whether it genuinely restored trust.

In other words, the data tells them the process is working, but says nothing about whether the experience is.

According to Deloitte, only 38 percent of executives say they have personally walked through their company's service recovery processes in the past year. That means more than half of the people in charge of delivering customer value haven't experienced their own organization's definition of "making it right."

That's not just operational blindness. That's a leadership failure.

RESOLUTION IS NOT A CHECKBOX

In most companies, a problem is considered resolved once it's removed from the queue. But for customers, resolution is rarely about a status update or an automated email. It's about outcome. It's about whether they were heard, whether they felt seen, whether someone made it right without making them work for it.

When customers say, "No one helped me," what they often mean is, "No one took ownership." When they say, "I had to repeat myself five times," they're not just frustrated by inefficiency—they're expressing a deeper disappointment: This company doesn't care enough to connect the dots.

This is where leadership must pause. Because if you're closing tickets without restoring trust, you're solving for volume—not value.

COMPLEXITY AT THE TOP, CONSEQUENCES AT THE BOTTOM

One of the biggest reasons resolution breaks down is that the people designing processes are far removed from their impact. Executives approve tech stacks that don't integrate. They greenlight rules that serve risk management but confuse frontline agents. They mandate productivity metrics that discourage real ownership.

To the C-suite, these decisions feel strategic. Controlled. Risk-balanced.

But on the front lines, they feel like a maze. A series of constraints that force well-meaning agents to say, "Sorry, I can't help you with that," instead of, "Let me make this right."

And for the customer, it doesn't matter whether the failure came from tech, policy, or training. What they remember is the experience. They remember the feeling of being passed off, of not being important enough for someone to follow through. And that feeling doesn't just affect one transaction—it affects every future decision about whether to do business with you again.

THE CULTURE OF "HANDLED"

When leaders are insulated from the reality of broken resolution, a dangerous phrase begins to emerge in corporate vocabulary: "We're handling it."

It becomes the catch-all response to issues that surface from escalations, social media blow-ups, or even direct board-level feedback. But what does "handled" really mean? Did the issue get closed? Did someone follow up? Was the root cause addressed? Or was the customer just offered a gift card and quietly removed from the complaint queue?

If senior leaders never follow up to ask those questions—if they never feel the urgency to walk the resolution journey themselves—then "handled" simply means out of sight, out of mind.

And in a business world where customers have more options, more influence, and more channels to amplify their voice than ever before, that kind of detachment is no longer survivable.

LEADERSHIP MUST RECLAIM RESPONSIBILITY FOR RESOLUTION

Fixing the resolution problem is not about investing in more tech, or adding headcount, or drafting better email templates. It starts with something far more fundamental: leadership accountability.

It requires executives to walk the customer journey—especially when it breaks. To listen in on support calls. To read transcripts. To ask why the same complaint keeps surfacing. And most importantly, to ask not "Did we close it?" but "Did we make it right?"

That's what customers want. That's what employees want. And that's what defines companies that earn loyalty—not just on good days, but on bad ones.

COMPANIES GETTING IT RIGHT

THEY DON'T JUST SOLVE THE PROBLEM—THEY TURN IT INTO A MOMENT OF TRUST

Most companies claim to be customer-centric—right up until something goes wrong. That's when the real brand shows up.

In those moments, some organizations hide behind process, policy, or platforms. Others step up and deliver what every customer wants most:

someone who owns the issue, acts quickly, and makes it right without making them jump through hoops.

What separates the best from the rest isn't their product. It's not even their people. It's what they empower those people to do—especially when a customer is frustrated, disappointed, or on the edge of walking away.

The following companies aren't perfect. But they've built cultures where resolution is not an obligation—it's an opportunity. They've operationalized what most leaders only talk about: trust, accountability, and care when it counts most.

RITZ-CARLTON: THE ART OF EMPOWERED ELEGANCE

At the Ritz-Carlton, you don't need to ask for the manager. The person you're speaking with is the solution.

Their famous service model authorizes every employee—from housekeeping to bell staff—to spend up to $2,000 per guest per incident to resolve an issue. No approvals. No forms. No delays. That level of trust doesn't just speed up recovery. It signals that every employee is a full representative of the brand.

And they use that power well.

If a guest mentions a missed housekeeping service, they might return from dinner to find their room turned down, a handwritten apology note, and a bottle of wine. If a traveler's luggage is lost in transit, it's not uncommon for a Ritz team member to personally shop for necessities while the airline scrambles. They don't just fix the problem. They respond with care—and precision.

The lesson here isn't about luxury. It's about standards. Ritz-Carlton understands that in moments of service failure, memorability is forged not by the absence of problems, but by the elegance and decisiveness of the response.

SPOTIFY: TECH AT THE FRONT, HUMANITY IN THE MIDDLE

Spotify operates in a fast-paced, digital-native space. It's the kind of company that could easily fall into the trap of over automating its support—burying customers in bots, menus, and self-service links.

Spotify has built one of the most frictionless digital support models in the subscription economy. And yet, when a customer hits a wall—whether it's a billing issue, an account lockout, or a family plan glitch—a human steps in, fully equipped to fix it.

What sets Spotify apart is that its resolution path doesn't reset the conversation. Customers aren't asked to reexplain the issue or navigate a new system. The transition from self-service to human support is seamless, and reps are trained to pick up the thread immediately.

There is no generic script. There's just someone saying, "Here's what I see. Let's fix it now."

Spotify understands that the modern customer doesn't want to talk to someone instead of using technology. They want to talk to someone when the technology fails. And when that happens, resolution isn't optional—it's a moment to reaffirm that the platform is powered by people who care.

L.L.BEAN: WHEN VALUES OUTLAST TRENDS

L.L.Bean doesn't rely on a tech stack to deliver resolution. It relies on something rarer: a 110-year-old promise that the customer always comes first.

Long before "CX" became an initialism, L.L.Bean had a reputation for doing the right thing. Its original guarantee—"If you're not 100 percent satisfied, return it anytime for a full refund"—wasn't a marketing line. It was a company philosophy. And while that policy has evolved slightly in recent years, the spirit remains untouched.

What makes L.L.Bean remarkable is not how often things go wrong—but how little friction there is when they do. Customers don't need to fight for a return, provide proof of defect, or argue over warranty coverage.

They don't need to rehearse a case or escalate to be taken seriously. They're met with, "We'll take care of it."

It's not just hassle-free. It's heart-forward.

When you return something to L.L.Bean, you don't leave feeling like you got away with something. You leave feeling like you were treated with dignity—as someone the company wants to keep for life, not just for the season.

And in a world increasingly driven by policies designed to protect the company from the customer, L.L.Bean has built enduring loyalty by doing the opposite.

RESOLUTION AS A COMPETITIVE WEAPON

Ritz-Carlton. Spotify. L.L.Bean.

Three very different industries. Three very different models. But one unshakable truth:

They treat customer issues as a test of the relationship—and they pass it, every time.

They don't delegate resolution to policy. They don't view it as a cost center. They build cultures where the answer isn't, "We'll escalate that," but rather, "We'll make it right—right now."

And they win because of it.

Not because they avoid mistakes—but because they own them when they happen. They recover with speed, with empathy, and with intent. And in doing so, they turn potential critics into evangelists.

That's the real benchmark. Not whether you get it right every time. But whether your customer believes you will do right by them when things inevitably go wrong.

THE FIX: VISIBILITY, SIMPLICITY, ACCOUNTABILITY

STOP MANAGING RESOLUTION AS A QUEUE. START OWNING IT AS A COMMITMENT.

If you've ever had to chase a company to fix something that was clearly their fault—a billing error, a broken product, a service failure—then you know what bad resolution feels like. It's not just frustrating. It's dehumanizing. It makes you question whether the brand ever cared about your business in the first place.

Companies that get resolution wrong often think they've done their part because they responded. Because the ticket was logged. Because the SLA clock stopped ticking. But customers aren't judging you by how quickly you acknowledged the problem—they're judging you by how thoroughly, and how thoughtfully, you resolved it.

To truly fix this, leaders must abandon the illusion that resolution is a task. It's not. It's a trust event. And it demands something more than metrics. It demands visibility, simplicity, and accountability—not as buzzwords, but as operating principles.

MAKE THE PROBLEM VISIBLE—FROM THE INSIDE OUT

The most dangerous resolution failures are the ones leaders never see. Not because they didn't happen—but because they didn't escalate. No one screamed. No one went viral. The customer just disappeared. Quietly. Permanently.

Executives look at closed cases and assume success. They see resolution rates and time-to-close and think, "We're doing well." But what they don't see is what the customer experienced: the three transfers, the reexplaining, the scripted apologies, the promise that someone would follow up—and never did.

Visibility means cutting through the illusion of service performance. It means listening to call recordings. Watching chat logs. Mystery shopping your own support. Sitting with frontline agents and asking, "What are you not empowered to do today that would fix 80 percent of your tickets?"

McKinsey reports that companies measuring entire customer journeys—not just isolated touchpoints—see up to a 20 percent boost in satisfaction and a 15 percent drop in service costs. Why? Because they see the gaps others ignore. They solve what actually matters.

Visibility isn't a report. It's a willingness to experience your own processes the way customers do. Not in a workshop. In the wild.

SIMPLIFY THE JOURNEY—OR WATCH YOUR CUSTOMERS LEAVE

When a customer has to work hard to fix your mistake, they're not thinking about your internal routing structure or org chart. They're thinking, "This brand does not respect my time."

Complex resolution paths often emerge from internal design: workflows optimized to balance queues, protect policies, and enforce controls. But every time you force a customer through another form, another agent, another delay, you're sending a message: The process matters more than you do.

The brands that retain loyalty don't just respond faster—they remove the steps that never needed to exist.

If your agent knows the customer's issue, let them solve it without escalation. If the customer already submitted a photo, stop asking them to explain the problem again. If you need to approve a refund, do it in real time—not in two weeks.

Customers don't want to escalate. They don't want to complain. They want a resolution that matches the simplicity of the problem. And if you can't deliver that, they'll walk—not because of what went wrong, but because of how hard you made it to make it right.

Simplification isn't a UX initiative. It's a leadership decision.

ESTABLISH REAL ACCOUNTABILITY—NOT JUST A CHAIN OF CUSTODY

Here's the silent killer in most resolution models: Everyone touches the issue, but no one owns it.

A case gets routed. A ticket gets updated. An email is sent. A callback is scheduled. And still, the problem persists. Because no one is responsible for closing the loop—not just procedurally, but emotionally.

Accountability means assigning end-to-end ownership for customer outcomes. It means a single person or team sees the issue through, regardless of how many systems, departments, or approvals are involved. It means someone has the authority and the expectation to follow through—not just check a box.

And accountability isn't just about escalation. It's about empathy-backed authority. The ability to say, "This shouldn't have happened—and I'm going to take care of it."

That's what resolution looks like when it's done right. It's not a back-and-forth. It's a baton that doesn't get dropped.

As one customer-centric COO put it: "The case is resolved when the customer stops thinking about it—not when we stop working on it."

That's the standard. That's the bar.

And it only happens when resolution is treated not as a handoff—but as a promise. One that someone is fully accountable for keeping.

RESOLUTION IS RETENTION. PERIOD.

When customers reach out with a problem, they're not just looking for an answer—they're looking for proof.

Proof that your brand stands behind what it sells.

Proof that they matter after the sale is made.

Proof that their time and trust are still worth something.

And too often, companies fail that test.

Not because they don't care. But because they've allowed resolution to become a series of transactions instead of a moment of truth.

They've wrapped it in scripts. They've buried it in escalations. They've passed it from desk to desk until the customer gives up.

And here's what leadership often forgets: When a customer stops pursuing resolution, it's not because the issue is fixed. It's because the relationship is broken.

In that moment, you haven't just lost a sale—you've lost belief. You've told the customer, whether you meant to or not: You're not important enough for us to fix this. That message doesn't show up in your dashboards. But it shows up in your churn. It shows up in your brand perception. And it shows up when your former customers talk about you to others.

Here's the hard truth: The best products in the world can't save you from unresolved problems. The most beautiful brand campaigns won't clean up the feeling of being dismissed. And the most optimized service flows won't matter if no one owns the outcome when something goes wrong.

Resolution is not a support function. It's a strategic differentiator. It's where loyalty is tested—and either reinforced or erased. The companies that win aren't the ones who avoid mistakes. They're the ones who take responsibility fast, fix it without friction, and restore trust with intention.

Because when you get resolution right, customers don't just forgive you—they believe in you.

And when you get it wrong? They never come back.

Key Takeaways

1. Resolution Isn't About Process—It's About Perception

Closing a ticket doesn't mean the problem is solved. If the customer still feels ignored, burdened, or dismissed, the issue isn't resolved—it's just logged. Resolution must restore trust, not just complete workflow.

2. Ownership Wins Loyalty—Handoffs Kill It

Customers don't leave because something went wrong. They leave because no one owned the fix. Empower your people to solve the issue fully, the first time. And if it requires escalation, assign real accountability—not a revolving door.

3. Every Unresolved Problem Is a Churn Signal—and a Brand Moment

When a customer reaches out with an issue, they're giving you a second chance. Failing to make it right doesn't just lose a sale—it loses the relationship. Resolution is not a cost center. It's a loyalty engine. Treat it like one.

CHAPTER 10

"Customers Want You to Know Them"

Marcus had flown with the same airline for nearly eight years. Mostly for work—enough to earn Gold status, but not enough to feel like a VIP. He didn't expect much anymore. He traveled efficiently, skipped the frills, and knew the gate routine by heart.

But on one particularly exhausting trip—delayed departure, tight connection, missed dinner—he arrived at his hotel late and opened the airline app to rebook his return.

There, at the top of the screen, was a simple message:

"Welcome back, Marcus. We've preselected your favorite seat for your return flight. Want to confirm it?" One tap. Done.

No upcharges. No unnecessary steps. No forced upsells. Just a quiet acknowledgment that someone, somewhere, had paid attention. Someone remembered that he always preferred an aisle seat in the second-to-last row. Someone made it easier, without him having to ask.

He didn't post about it. He didn't call customer service to thank them. But in that moment, something changed—he felt seen.

And that small act of personalization—no fireworks, no grand gesture—earned something far more valuable than the next ticket. It earned his loyalty. Not because the company knew who he was, but because it showed why that knowledge mattered.

Personalization should feel helpful, not like surveillance. This is what customers want. Not just to be marketed to. Not just to be tracked. They want to be recognized in ways that help, not interrupt. That simplify, not pressure. That say, "We know you," without ever having to say it aloud.

It's not the data that builds trust. It's what you do with it.

THE PERSONALIZATION PARADOX

CUSTOMERS WANT TO BE KNOWN—BUT ON THEIR TERMS

Personalization is no longer a nice-to-have—it's expected. When done right, it makes customers feel seen, valued, and understood. It removes friction. It increases relevance. It saves time. And in today's experience economy, those things matter more than ever.

In fact, most customers welcome a brand's ability to recognize them—as long as it makes their lives easier. A returning shopper doesn't want to reenter their shipping address. A loyal flier doesn't want to pick their preferred seat every time. A repeat guest shouldn't have to remind the hotel they prefer a quiet room away from the elevator.

According to a report from McKinsey, 71 percent of consumers expect companies to deliver personalized interactions—and 76 percent get frustrated when that doesn't happen. This isn't simply about targeting. It's about creating a sense of continuity—an unspoken acknowledgment that says: We remember you, and we're here to make things easier because of it.

But the paradox emerges quickly.

Because while customers want to be known, they don't want to feel tracked. They want the benefits of personalization without the discomfort of surveillance. And that line—the one between helpful and intrusive—is not just thin. It's moving. What feels intuitive today might feel invasive tomorrow. What one customer sees as thoughtful, another sees as overreach.

Too often, brands race to implement every available personalization feature without stepping back to ask the one question that matters most: Does this feel respectful?

Customers want relevance. They want their loyalty to be recognized. They want a faster path to what they need. But they also want agency. They want to opt in—not be dragged in. They want to feel known—not watched. And above all, they want the experience to feel like it's for them, not just about them.

When personalization becomes a tactic instead of a value, it starts to backfire. What once felt tailored begins to feel transactional. What once enhanced the relationship begins to erode it.

This is the paradox: Personalization is most effective when it disappears. When it fades into the background and quietly improves the customer journey without calling attention to itself.

The best brands know this. They don't confuse recognition with intrusion. They build trust by personalizing the experience in ways that feel natural, earned, and optional—never assumed.

Because in today's marketplace, the brands that win aren't just the ones that know the customer. They're the ones who understand when not to show it.

WHEN PERSONALIZATION FEELS CREEPY, NOT CONVENIENT

WHEN THE EXPERIENCE STOPS FEELING TAILORED AND STARTS FEELING TRACKED

Personalization is not optional anymore. It's the new baseline.

In a digital-first world, customers expect more than one-size-fits-all experiences. They expect the companies they do business with to know their preferences, anticipate their needs, and make relevant suggestions without requiring them to start over every time. According to McKinsey, companies that excel at personalization generate 40 percent more revenue than those that don't. Customers spend more, engage longer, and churn less when they feel like the brand gets them.

When done right, personalization feels like ease. It feels like the barista who remembers your order. The app that loads your favorite settings before you ask. The airline that knows you'd rather sit in an aisle than by the window. These touches are quiet, useful, and—most importantly—earned.

But the line between relevance and overreach is dangerously thin. And far too many brands cross it without realizing it—until it's too late.

It often starts with good intent: serve the customer better by anticipating what they want. But what begins as thoughtful often becomes intrusive when personalization is rushed, unfiltered, or uninvited.

It's the online retailer who sends an email five minutes after you abandon your cart—not just with the item, but with three others you looked at and never clicked.

It's the streaming service that recommends content based on a private genre search you watched once, late at night, alone.

It's the healthcare portal that uses behavioral data to recommend a treatment path you never asked for, and weren't emotionally prepared to receive.

These aren't just examples of marketing misfires. They're moments when personalization stops serving the customer—and starts unnerving them.

And the worst part? It happens fast. One misstep, one ill-timed message, one eerie insight, and the entire dynamic changes. What felt like a relationship begins to feel like surveillance.

A 2022 Pew Research study found that 79 percent of US adults are concerned about how companies use their data, and 59 percent say they have very little or no understanding of what companies actually do with it.

This isn't an edge case. It's the norm. Consumers know their behavior is being tracked. What they're no longer tolerating is the opacity—the vague privacy policies, the auto-checked boxes, the sense that they're part of a machine they didn't consent to join.

The irony is that the very thing that makes personalization powerful—its precision—is also what makes it risky. The more specific it becomes, the more obvious it is that someone, somewhere, is watching.

That's where the discomfort begins. Because customers don't want to feel like profiles. They want to feel like people. And people have boundaries. They want to be recognized, not dissected. Informed, not manipulated. Understood—not sold.

When personalization fails to consider those emotional boundaries, it doesn't just underperform. It damages trust. It makes customers hesitate before clicking, before sharing, before coming back. And that hesitation is the real cost.

Because while companies obsess over conversion rates and targeting precision, what they should be measuring is customer confidence. How safe does the customer feel in this relationship? How much agency do they believe they have? How likely are they to share more, not less, the next time?

That's the ultimate ROI of personalization done right—a customer who's not just willing to be known, but who wants to be.

But get it wrong, and that willingness evaporates. And with it goes the loyalty, the engagement, and the data you worked so hard to earn in the first place.

Personalization is still one of the most powerful tools a brand can use. But power without judgment is dangerous. Relevance without consent is manipulation. And convenience without context becomes surveillance.

The best companies understand that personalization isn't a campaign. It's a contract. And it's built on a promise: We will use what we know to serve you—not to control you.

THE PRIVACY BACKLASH IS REAL—AND GROWING

CUSTOMERS ARE NO LONGER JUST SENSITIVE ABOUT PRIVACY—THEY'RE TAKING ACTION

The shift didn't happen all at once. But it's here now, unmistakable and accelerating.

Customers used to assume that data collection was the price of admission for digital convenience. They accepted tracking cookies, personalized ads, and behavioral nudges as part of the modern online experience. Most didn't read the fine print. Many didn't feel they had a choice.

But that era is over.

We've entered a new phase of consumer awareness—one where privacy isn't just a concern. It's a dealbreaker. And companies that fail to acknowledge that shift aren't just being outpaced by policy—they're being abandoned by their customers.

According to PwC, over 83 percent of consumers say they want more control over how their data is used, and over 60 percent say they would stop doing business with a company that mishandles their personal information.

THE TIPPING POINT: FROM PASSIVE CONSENT TO ACTIVE CONTROL

In the past, most brands operated on the assumption of implicit trust. If a user created an account or downloaded the app, that was enough. Privacy policies were dense, opt-outs were buried, and data collection defaulted to always on.

But customers are no longer passive.

They're questioning not just what data is collected—but why, how, and for whose benefit. They're installing tracker blockers. They're clearing cookies. They're reading reviews to see whether companies respect opt-out requests. They're asking, Do I trust this brand with my digital self?

The modern consumer has moved from resignation to resistance. And that's a shift leaders cannot afford to ignore.

REGULATION IS CATCHING UP—AND CATCHING BRANDS OFF GUARD

The regulatory landscape is evolving rapidly. GDPR in Europe was just the beginning. The California Consumer Privacy Act (CCPA), the Virginia Consumer Data Protection Act (VCDPA), and similar laws in Colorado, Connecticut, and beyond have begun to redefine what "consent" means—and what accountability looks like.

But legislation isn't just about fines. It's about signaling a new expectation: Privacy is no longer a compliance issue—it's a leadership obligation.

Companies that treat privacy as a checkbox will be left behind. Not just because the rules are changing, but because customers are watching.

And the real risk isn't regulatory. It's reputational.

When a customer sees a company mishandle their data—a breach, a non-consensual tracking ad, a mysteriously personalized message that wasn't supposed to exist—they don't file a complaint. They disappear. And they take others with them.

A 2023 Cisco Consumer Privacy Survey revealed that 76 percent of global consumers say they would not buy from a company they do not trust to protect their data. In other words, trust is not just a feeling—it's a revenue stream.

DATA IS NOT A RIGHT. IT'S A PRIVILEGE.

The companies that get this right operate with a fundamentally different mindset.

They understand that customer data isn't an entitlement. It's earned trust. And it can be taken away—not just by the click of a "delete my data" button, but by the erosion of belief that the company is acting in good faith.

This is where many brands go wrong. They focus on what the law allows instead of what the customer expects. They collect everything because they can, not because they should. They confuse capability with permission—and they pay for it.

The result isn't just churn. It's silence. A disengaged customer who no longer opens your emails, logs into your app, or shares any behavior that could make your systems smarter. You haven't just lost access to their data—you've lost their relationship.

PRIVACY IS THE NEW BRAND DIFFERENTIATOR

In a marketplace flooded with messages, features, and claims, customers are seeking something more fundamental: safety.

They want to know that they can browse, buy, and engage without wondering who's listening. They want transparency not buried in a twelve-page policy—but built into the experience.

This is where leading brands are pulling ahead. Not by rejecting personalization, but by redefining the terms of engagement.

Apple now leads with privacy in its marketing—positioning itself not just as a product company, but as a steward of personal data. Brands like DuckDuckGo, ProtonMail, and Signal are growing not because of flashy features, but because of a singular promise: We protect you.

And even mainstream brands like Target and CVS have redesigned parts of their digital journeys to clearly communicate what data they collect and why—and, more importantly, to let customers opt out without penalty.

These companies aren't just avoiding risk. They're building competitive advantage.

Because trust is now a differentiator. And privacy is the foundation that trust stands on.

THE CX AND C-SUITE LEADERSHIP BREAKDOWN

WHEN DATA STRATEGY OUTPACES CUSTOMER STRATEGY, TRUST IS THE FIRST CASUALTY

It's easy for executives to talk about customer experience. It's harder to operationalize it when data, marketing automation, and commercial pressure are all pulling in the opposite direction.

Inside boardrooms and digital strategy meetings, "personalization" is often a buzzword that gets misinterpreted as "use as much data as possible to drive conversion." And so the conversations drift quickly toward tools and tactics: real-time tracking, next-best-action engines, advanced segmentation. The assumption is that if you can personalize more, you should—because customers expect it.

But that assumption is flawed. Because what customers actually expect is not more personalization. They expect better personalization—built on transparency, consent, and care.

That nuance gets lost at the top. And when it does, the organization doesn't just risk overstepping boundaries. It actively undermines the very trust its brand is built on.

DATA IS OFTEN WEAPONIZED WITHOUT INTENTIONAL GOVERNANCE

Many executives treat customer data as a raw material to be mined. The more granular, the better. But what they forget is that behind every behavioral tag, clickstream, or inferred preference is a human being—someone who may not realize how much they've already shared, or how deeply they're being tracked.

What starts as a customer intelligence program quickly morphs into behavioral surveillance. Not because anyone intended harm, but because no one built in restraint.

The incentive structures inside most companies are designed to reward performance, not prudence. The marketing team is rewarded for conversion. The data team is rewarded for scale. The product team is rewarded for engagement. So everyone leans in—aggressively—to extract more insight, deliver more customization, and trigger more outcomes.

But no one's rewarded for asking, "Is this too much?"

When the strategy is optimized for output, but not for empathy, you're not serving the customer—you're profiling them.

THE RISK OF LEADERSHIP ABSTRACTION

Senior leaders rarely experience personalization as their customers do. They don't see their own data profiles. They aren't targeted by their own remarketing campaigns. They don't receive the late-night follow-up messages triggered by one abandoned cart.

Instead, they review reports. They see uplift curves, open rates, and drop-off analysis. They're removed from the emotion of the experience. They manage personalization as a spreadsheet—not as a relationship.

This abstraction creates blind spots. Leaders become enthusiastic about "using every signal" without ever asking how it feels to be on the receiving end. They approve campaigns that use language like, "We noticed you haven't visited us in a while," without realizing that the customer didn't ask to be watched.

And because most complaints don't make it to their level—because discomfort isn't always expressed as outrage—they assume that silence means satisfaction.

But in truth, silence often means retreat. And when customers retreat, they don't come back with feedback. They just stop engaging.

Training Investment vs. Customer Satisfaction by Industry

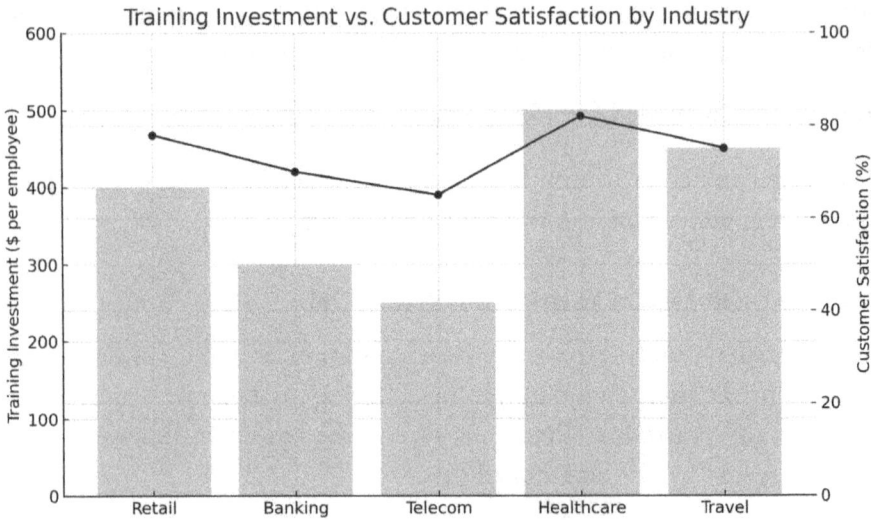

Source: ATD 2023 State of the Industry; Forrester CX Index 2023.

INTERNAL FRAGMENTATION FUELS EXTERNAL CREEPINESS

Personalization rarely lives in one part of the organization. Marketing owns messaging. Digital owns channels. Data teams manage profiles. Legal signs off on policy. Product teams control in-app recommendations. Each team thinks they're doing something minor—a small optimization here, a smart nudge there.

But the customer experiences all of it at once.

They don't distinguish between a marketing email that references an old browsing session and a product alert that assumes a need they never stated. They just feel watched. And worse, misunderstood.

This is where personalization breaks down—when teams are coordinating data, but not coordinating intent.

Without a shared philosophy around why and how customer data is used, companies become a patchwork of silent overreach. And by the time someone in leadership realizes how it all feels to the customer, the damage has already been done.

THE ROLE OF CX LEADERSHIP—AND WHY IT'S OFTEN MISSING

Customer experience leaders should be the conscience of data-driven innovation. They should be the voice in the room saying, "Yes, this is clever—but will it feel right?" They should be asking how it lands emotionally, not just how it performs tactically.

But too often, CX is still marginalized—viewed as a reactive function or a service center. They're consulted after the build, after the segmentation, after the campaign has launched. And when customers complain, then they're asked to step in.

This reactive posture keeps CX from influencing the core decisions that define how data is used. And it keeps companies from asking the most important design question of all: Are we building trust or borrowing it?

Because if you're borrowing it—if your entire personalization strategy is dependent on assumptions, proxies, and invisible tracking—you'd better hope the customer never finds out how it works. And that's a losing game.

DATA ETHICS IS NOW A BOARDROOM COMPETENCY

The most progressive organizations understand that personalization is not just about algorithms—it's about values.

They treat data stewardship not as a policy—but as a principle. They recognize that trust is a strategic asset. And they put guardrails in place to ensure that what's possible is always balanced against what's appropriate.

These companies elevate privacy conversations to the C-suite. They bring CX, legal, and data together in planning—not just in response. They ask hard questions, and they embed customer trust into the same dashboards that track revenue and engagement.

Because they know that data is not just a competitive advantage—it's a fragile social contract.

And if you break it, no amount of personalization will win the customer back.

COMPANIES GETTING IT RIGHT

PERSONALIZATION THAT RESPECTS THE LINE— AND BUILDS LOYALTY BECAUSE OF IT

The best personalization doesn't feel like technology. It feels like consideration.

It's the brand that anticipates what you need—not just because it can, but because it knows when to stop. It's the subtle opt-in, the message that arrives at the right time in the right tone, the offer that makes your life easier without making you wonder, How did they know that?

While some companies stumble into the trap of overcollection and overexposure, others have chosen a smarter path: personalization that's grounded in transparency, guided by ethics, and designed with the customer's emotional comfort in mind.

Here are three such brands that show how it's done—and done well.

REI: PERSONALIZATION THROUGH PARTICIPATION, NOT SURVEILLANCE

REI doesn't guess what you want. It asks.

The outdoor co-op uses preference-based data, purchase history, and opt-in content engagement to tailor experiences for members—but always with full visibility and consent. Their product recommendations aren't derived from tracking your every move across the internet. They're based on what you told them you care about: hiking vs. cycling, weekend backpacking vs. alpine climbing.

The company excels at making personalization feel like a partnership. Their emails don't say, "We noticed you browsing tents." They say, "Because you told us you love backcountry trips, here's what's new in lightweight gear." It feels collaborative—not creepy.

What makes REI's approach even stronger is that it's embedded in a brand promise. As a member-owned co-op, customers are treated like contributors—not data points. That mindset shapes everything from communication tone to product curation to digital experience design.

And customers respond accordingly: not just with clicks, but with loyalty born from trust.

BANK OF AMERICA: HIGH-TOUCH PERSONALIZATION WITHOUT OVERSTEPPING

In a heavily regulated industry like banking, trust isn't a feature—it's a prerequisite. Bank of America has built one of the most advanced personalization ecosystems in financial services, but it does so within firm boundaries and a strong privacy posture.

Through its app and digital channels, Bank of America provides what it calls "life-stage-based guidance." That might mean prompting a customer to open a 529 college savings plan based on age and savings behavior—but never with invasive assumptions or hyperpersonalized ads that reveal sensitive financial activity.

Its virtual assistant, Erica, offers proactive help—reminding users about upcoming bills, suggesting budgeting tools, or flagging unusual transactions. But these nudges are carefully tuned to feel helpful, not heavy-handed.

What sets B of A apart is its restraint. It rarely feels like it's trying to sell you something. Instead, it behaves like a well-informed adviser who offers suggestions only when it's appropriate. The customer retains agency—and that's the foundation of long-term trust.

NORDSTROM: HUMANIZED DIGITAL ENGAGEMENT WITH BUILT-IN CHOICE

In retail, personalization often falls into two camps: creepy or clunky. But Nordstrom strikes a rare balance—combining digital precision with human grace.

Their online experience integrates data seamlessly: past purchases, sizing preferences, and browsing history inform curated looks and suggestions.

But the way that personalization is delivered is what stands out. It's not forced. It's not pushy. And it never feels like you're being watched.

One standout: Their "Style Board" feature lets customers collaborate with personal stylists virtually. You opt in. You share preferences. And Nordstrom matches you with a stylist who builds customized outfit suggestions—which you can accept, ignore, or refine.

It's personalization that feels like service, not targeting.

And that same philosophy extends into their physical stores. Associates use customer data only when appropriate, often referencing past purchases or styles saved in a shopper's account—but always with permission and context. Nothing feels assumed. Everything feels thoughtful.

The result? Nordstrom has become one of the few legacy retailers that has successfully blended digital personalization with human connection—and done so without crossing the line into overreach.

WHAT THEY ALL UNDERSTAND

REI, Bank of America, and Nordstrom operate in vastly different industries. But they share a core belief: Personalization is earned, not assumed.

They don't treat data as leverage. They treat it as a privilege—something the customer grants, not something they mine.

Their personalization strategies aren't about showing off technical capability. They're about demonstrating emotional intelligence: knowing when to recommend, when to hold back, and how to let the customer guide the level of intimacy in the relationship.

Most importantly, they don't just collect data. They explain it. They provide choices. They offer opt-outs and controls without friction. And in doing so, they build something most companies chase through dashboards and algorithms:

THE FIX: RELEVANCE, RESPECT, RESPONSIBILITY

PERSONALIZATION WITHOUT TRUST ISN'T PERSONALIZATION—IT'S JUST TARGETING

Personalization can be powerful. But only if it's grounded in a relationship the customer actually wants.

When brands get personalization wrong, it's not because they lack the right data or tools. It's because they ignore the emotional foundation that makes personalization work: the customer's willingness to be known. That willingness is not automatic—it's earned. And earning it requires more than capability. It requires relevance, respect, and responsibility.

RELEVANCE: PERSONALIZE WITH PURPOSE, NOT FOR PERFORMANCE

Just because you can personalize doesn't mean you should. And just because you have data doesn't mean it's meaningful.

Relevance means focusing personalization on things the customer actually wants. It's not about triggering every campaign that matches a behavior. It's about asking: Will this make their experience better, faster, more thoughtful, or more convenient?

It's not about what serves the business. It's about what serves the customer. A helpful reminder. A faster checkout. A meaningful recommendation. These are acts of service—not surveillance.

Leaders must demand a shift in mindset across marketing, digital, and product teams: less automation, more intention. Less "next best action," more "right time, right reason."

When personalization is driven by purpose—not pressure—it becomes a differentiator instead of a liability.

RESPECT: MAKE CONSENT A DESIGN PRINCIPLE

Most privacy policies are written for lawyers. Most opt-in flows are designed to be ignored. And most customers feel like they're being asked to trust companies that aren't willing to explain why they're asking for their data in the first place.

That has to change.

Respect means making data collection, personalization, and privacy visible, explainable, and optional.

That doesn't just mean putting a checkbox on your site. It means clearly showing what you're collecting, what you'll use it for, and what the customer gets in return. It means offering opt-out paths that don't feel like punishment. It means treating consent as a design standard—not a compliance line item.

And it means aligning the customer experience with your brand voice. If your company claims to be about trust, simplicity, or human connection—your privacy and personalization practices should reflect that.

Customers don't just want to say yes. They want to understand what they're saying yes to. If your personalization strategy can't pass that test, it's not ready.

RESPONSIBILITY: TREAT DATA LIKE REPUTATION—BECAUSE IT IS

Every piece of customer data your company holds is a reflection of trust.

Responsibility means treating that data like an extension of your reputation. You wouldn't mishandle someone's credit card. Don't mishandle their preferences, habits, or behaviors either.

Too many companies treat data as an exhaust pipe—something to gather, segment, and weaponize for growth. But the smartest companies treat it like a shared contract.

That means governing how data is accessed internally. That means empowering teams to ask why a data point is being used before deploying it in a campaign. That means integrating ethical checks into your product development process—and giving CX and privacy teams real authority to halt initiatives that overstep.

Responsibility also means being proactive about what happens when things go wrong. If there's a breach, a misuse, or a misstep in personalization—own it fast, explain it clearly, and show your work to fix it.

Because the only thing more damaging than over personalizing is pretending you didn't.

THE FIX BEGINS WITH THE QUESTIONS YOU ASK

When your teams design a campaign, a product flow, or a new data strategy—are they asking the right questions?

- Who benefits from this personalization—us, or the customer?
- Is the customer aware this data is being used?
- If this message showed up at the wrong time or in the wrong context, how would it feel?
- Are we giving the customer a meaningful way to say no?

These are the questions that separate ethical, effective personalization from the kind that drives customers away.

The future isn't more personalization. It's smarter personalization—guided by empathy, delivered with transparency, and powered by trust.

CUSTOMERS WANT TO BE KNOWN—BUT ON THEIR TERMS

Personalization is not the problem. The lack of discretion is.

Customers are not rejecting relevance. They're rejecting the assumption that access to their behavior means permission to act on it. They're pushing back on being studied without being respected. And they're walking away from brands that confuse insight with entitlement.

They want to be remembered. Not profiled.

They want experiences tailored to their preferences. Not algorithms that expose their behaviors.

They want to opt in—not be backed into a corner.

What used to be considered personalization is now being redefined as performance marketing. And what companies used to call "smart targeting" now often gets called out as invasive.

This is where leadership must evolve.

The brands that win tomorrow aren't the ones with the most data—they're the ones who know how to use it responsibly. Who know when to step forward with a helpful suggestion—and when to step back and let the customer lead.

Because the question has changed. It's no longer "Can you personalize?"

It's "Do I trust you to?"

Every email you send, every recommendation you push, every "you might like" banner that follows a customer across their digital life—it all speaks to one deeper truth: How well do you understand the boundary between helpful and presumptive?

Get it right, and customers will share more. Stay longer. Buy more often.

Get it wrong, and they won't just ignore you—they'll silence you.

Personalization done well feels like recognition.

Done poorly, it feels like surveillance.

And once your brand crosses that line, no amount of apology or opt-out button will earn that trust back.

In the end, customers want to feel like the experience was built for them.

But they want to know they were invited into it—not tracked into it.

Key Takeaways

1. Personalization Must Be Earned, Not Assumed

Customers expect relevance—but only when it's rooted in transparency, choice, and consent. Without trust, personalization becomes intrusive. Treat data access as a privilege, not a right.

2. Ethical Data Use Is a Leadership Issue, Not a Legal One

Privacy and personalization aren't departmental responsibilities. They are brand-defining decisions that start in the C-suite. When customer trust erodes, it's not a marketing failure—it's a leadership failure.

3. The Line Between Helpful and Creepy Is a Moving Target—Lead with Judgment

Context, timing, and tone matter. Effective personalization feels like being understood. Poor personalization feels like being watched. Build systems that can do both—but cultures that know the difference.

PART TWO

The Fix

CHAPTER 11

Measuring the Right Things—
Beyond the Typical Metrics

"WE HAVE GREAT NUMBERS. SO WHY ARE
WE STILL LOSING CUSTOMERS?"

It's the quiet panic that plays out in executive meetings across industries. The data is up. The reports are clean. NPS is trending in the right direction. CSAT is above target. First-call resolution is improving quarter over quarter. The CX team shares a dashboard filled with positive signals.

And yet, customers are leaving.

They're not raging. They're not protesting. They're just...gone. Quiet churn. Silent drop-off. Reduced engagement. Fewer renewals. And for some reason, it's not showing up where leadership expects it. That's because most companies aren't measuring the right things. They're measuring the easy things.

WHAT'S EASY?

Scores. Time stamps. Survey checkboxes. Operational KPIs that look good in a meeting and fit neatly into a bar chart. Metrics that can be benchmarked, celebrated, and gamified. Metrics that tell you customers are fine—until they're not.

As Forrester has reported, while 73 percent of organizations say they use NPS as their primary CX measure, only 16 percent find it truly actionable. That's not just an execution issue. That's a strategic crisis hiding behind pretty numbers.

This is the illusion of insight: When the metrics tell you things are working, but the customer reality says otherwise. It's when your dashboard gets more attention than your front line. When you chase scores instead of solving problems. When you ask for feedback—and ignore what it actually means.

And over time, this illusion doesn't just mislead leaders. It reshapes incentives, fuels the wrong behaviors, and erodes trust from the inside out.

Because what gets measured gets managed. But what gets mis-measured gets misunderstood, misaligned, and quietly abandoned by the people you're trying to keep.

THE METRICS THAT DON'T TELL THE WHOLE STORY

WHY "GOOD NUMBERS" CAN MASK A BROKEN EXPERIENCE

NPS. CSAT. AHT. FCR.

These are the default metrics on every customer experience dashboard. They're familiar. Standardized. Executive-friendly. They produce scorecards, trendlines, and slide decks that suggest the brand is listening, tracking, improving.

And yet—they're not enough. And in some cases, they're dangerously misleading.

NET PROMOTER SCORE (NPS)

NPS asks a simple question: "How likely are you to recommend us?" And that simplicity is what made it so popular. It creates a benchmark. A number to chase. A north star.

But here's the problem: NPS is a lagging indicator. By the time it tells you something is wrong, the damage is already done. It also lacks context. A high NPS doesn't tell you why the customer is happy. A low NPS doesn't tell you what they expected. Worse, it's often measured at the wrong moments—like immediately after a support interaction, where a polite agent masks a painful process.

Even more problematic, companies game it. They prompt for nines and tens. They filter out negative responses. They incentivize teams to chase the number instead of improving the experience.

So what you get isn't loyalty. You get performance theater.

CUSTOMER SATISFACTION (CSAT)

CSAT is often tied to a specific interaction: "How satisfied were you with your recent experience?" It provides immediate feedback—and that's valuable.

But CSAT is limited. It doesn't account for cumulative frustration. It doesn't measure how many steps it took to get to that point. A customer can feel satisfied with the support agent but still deeply frustrated by the journey. You get a positive CSAT on the tenth call—but no insight into why it took ten calls in the first place.

AVERAGE HANDLE TIME (AHT)

AHT is beloved by operations teams. It shows how quickly agents are wrapping up interactions. It's easy to track, compare, and report. But what it often rewards is speed over substance.

AHT optimization encourages agents to rush. To close tickets instead of solving problems. To push customers out of the queue instead of through the solution. You may see short calls. But you may also see high repeat contacts, poor retention, and customers who feel like their time was disrespected, not saved.

FIRST-CALL RESOLUTION (FCR)

FCR is the idea that if you solve the problem the first time, the customer wins. That's true—if it's measured correctly. But FCR is often gamed. Teams mark issues "resolved" even when the customer hasn't confirmed it. Metrics show resolution, but customers feel like they're stuck in an endless loop.

FCR also misses whether the resolution actually lasted. A "first-call fix" that breaks a week later isn't a fix—it's a false positive.

THE REAL RISK: METRICS THAT MANAGE OPTICS, NOT OUTCOMES

The danger isn't in tracking these metrics. It's in treating them as truth without understanding what they ignore.

They don't measure emotional friction. They don't track how many customers gave up without responding to a survey. They don't reflect the cost of silence—when a customer chooses not to complain, but simply leaves.

And because they're easy to display, they're often weaponized. Teams get rewarded for green dashboards instead of red flags. Leaders feel good about direction instead of asking what's missing from the view.

You can't fix what you're not willing to measure honestly. Customers aren't reacting to your metrics. They're reacting to their experience.

WHAT YOU SHOULD BE MEASURING INSTEAD

IF YOU WANT TO KEEP CUSTOMERS, MEASURE WHAT FRUSTRATES THEM

Traditional CX metrics tell you what happened. But the best CX organizations don't just measure results—they measure resistance. They track how hard the customer had to push, how many steps it took, how many chances they gave before they gave up. Because customers don't leave over a single bad interaction. They leave when the entire experience starts to feel too hard and too hopeless.

The following signals don't always show up in the standard dashboard—but they should. Because they tell the real story of what it's like to do business with you.

- **Customer Effort Score (CES)**

  CES asks one powerful question: "How easy was it for you to resolve your issue?"

  Unlike CSAT or NPS, it doesn't focus on happiness or brand sentiment. It focuses on friction. It cuts through politeness and gets to the truth: Did we make this hard?

  Gartner research shows that lowering customer effort is the single strongest predictor of customer loyalty—more than delight or surprise.

  Low effort doesn't mean low touch. It means removing unnecessary steps, avoiding repeat contacts, and eliminating confusion. CES helps expose which parts of your process are designed for the business, not the customer.

- **Repeat Contact Rate (RCR)**

  You resolved it once—but did it stick?

  RCR measures how often customers have to reach out multiple times to solve the same issue. A company can claim high first-call resolution, but if repeat contact rate is also high, something's wrong. Maybe the root cause wasn't addressed. Maybe the "fix" created a new problem. Maybe no one followed up.

  High RCR means you're burning both customer trust and operational capacity. And it means your systems are optimizing for closure—not resolution.

- **Abandonment and Silent Drop-Off Rates**

  Sometimes the most dangerous signals are the ones that don't generate a contact or a complaint.

- How many customers bail during a self-service flow?
- How many start a chat, then close it without engaging?
- How many open a support article, scroll for ninety seconds, then leave without action?

These are signals of quiet frustration. They tell you when your experience was too complex, too vague, or too impersonal to be worth the effort. And yet, many companies don't track these moments. They track contacts not noncontacts. They reward deflection not resolution. That's a blind spot with consequences.

- **Churn Attribution by Experience Breakdown**

It's not enough to know who left. You need to know why.

When a customer churns, don't just log it as "natural attrition." Overlay their experience history. Were they part of a refund delay? Did they have an unresolved ticket? Did they browse cancellation terms multiple times before they walked?

Most companies conduct exit interviews like a checkbox. But great companies treat churn as a postmortem: a chance to learn, fix, and prevent. According to Deloitte, fewer than 30 percent of companies actively map churn to CX moments. That means 70 percent are walking blind into their next loss.

- **Policy Escalation and Exception Rates**

If your policies are working, exceptions should be rare. If you're constantly overriding them, your policies are the problem.

Tracking how often agents escalate a policy denial—or how often leaders approve exceptions—tells you whether your guardrails are designed to protect the customer or defend the company.

High exception rates mean your rules are out of step with reality.

THESE METRICS TELL A DIFFERENT STORY—THE REAL ONE

While traditional KPIs are clean and easy to present, they often miss the nuance that drives real emotion. Measuring effort, rework, abandonment, and escalations might be messier—but they're more honest.

They show you the pain points before they become PR problems.

They spotlight where trust is quietly breaking.

And they give you a roadmap to prevent the churn you never see coming.

Because if you want to understand your customer's experience, you can't just measure when they say something.

You have to measure what it took for them to say anything at all.

WHY THIS MATTERS

WHAT YOU MEASURE BECOMES THE CULTURE YOU BUILD

Metrics don't just inform decisions. They shape them. Over time, the numbers you choose to highlight become the behaviors your teams learn to chase.

If you measure speed, your people will move fast.

If you measure cost per contact, they'll cut corners.

If you celebrate high CSAT after long resolution paths, they'll optimize for politeness—not impact.

But if you measure what really matters—like effort, empathy, trust recovery, and unresolved friction—your teams will behave differently. They'll stop treating metrics as report cards and start treating them as navigation tools.

And that's when your culture shifts. From defensive to responsive. From reactive to strategic. From scorekeeping to story-hearing.

METRICS DON'T JUST REFLECT CULTURE—THEY CREATE IT

Your dashboards tell your teams what matters. Whether you intend to or not, your metrics say: "This is where we win," "This is where we're watching," and, "This is what leadership values most."

So when leadership continues to reward NPS lifts without examining how the score was earned… When performance reviews prioritize AHT over emotional intelligence…

When teams are praised for pushing deflections instead of resolving root causes…

You've created a culture of optics. One where success is gamed, not earned. That culture is exactly what customers feel—even if you don't.

MISALIGNED METRICS BECOME STRATEGIC RISK

Flawed measurement doesn't just impact the customer. It impacts resource allocation, talent retention, innovation priorities, and compliance exposure.

When the wrong KPIs are optimized:

- Product teams build enhancements that look good in demos but don't address real pain.
- Operations double down on automation that frustrates customers instead of serving them.
- CX teams are forced to "paint the dashboard green" while support queues are burning.

Meanwhile, your executives are making strategic bets based on data that's neat, but not true.

This is how brands lose their way—not from lack of intention, but from lack of honest insight.

THE LEADERSHIP MANDATE: GET CURIOUS ABOUT WHAT'S NOT ON THE CHART

If you're a CX leader, this is your moment to step up. Not just to report, but to reframe. Ask the uncomfortable questions: What are we not hearing because our metrics don't make space for it? What are we missing because we optimized for the wrong signal? What truths are buried under a good-looking score?

Because the answers won't come from a dashboard. They'll come from interrogating your assumptions. Customers will always tell you what they need—if you're willing to measure where it hurts.

CASE STUDY: SOUTHWEST AIRLINES

Southwest Airlines has long been known for its service-first culture. But even with its reputation for friendliness, the company faced a critical realization: Traditional CX metrics weren't keeping up with modern customer expectations—or modern operational demands.

Surveys came in too late. NPS was too abstract. CSAT told them what happened, but not why it happened or how to prevent it.

To fix that, Southwest turned to Qualtrics Experience Management (XM)—not as a dashboard tool, but as a system to fundamentally rethink how they listen to customers, interpret signals, and trigger action.

MOVING FROM METRICS TO MOMENTS

Southwest didn't stop using NPS or CSAT—but they stopped pretending those scores were enough. Instead, they built real-time feedback loops that captured what mattered most to the customer in the moment it happened:

- Was it hard to change a flight?
- Did the mobile app create friction at check-in?
- Was the gate agent empathetic or dismissive?
- Was the baggage delay acknowledged—or ignored?

These questions weren't answered weeks later in quarterly summaries. They were answered right there—during the journey—using automated prompts, natural language processing, and signal analysis from across digital and in-person touchpoints.

That's the difference: Southwest moved beyond surveys and into experience intelligence.

ACTIONABLE SIGNALS, DELIVERED IN REAL TIME

What made this shift powerful wasn't just smarter measurement—it was faster escalation.

If feedback indicated a surge in frustration at a particular airport, local leaders were alerted. If repeated complaints referenced the same app glitch, digital teams prioritized it. If customers felt stranded at the gate, someone got that feedback while the customer was still in the terminal.

This wasn't reactive CX. It was real-time recovery.

CX wasn't a function. It was a capability—woven into the operational rhythm of the business.

BEHAVIOR CHANGE AT EVERY LEVEL

Modern measurement didn't just change how data was captured. It changed how decisions were made.

- Station managers had better insight into what was going wrong at their location.
- Product teams saw real patterns in customer pain—not just stakeholder assumptions.
- Frontline agents received coaching based on real interactions and sentiment signals—not generic metrics.

The impact was cultural. It didn't just produce better dashboards. It created better instincts across the company.

As one Southwest executive put it: "We used to measure what was easy to report. Now we measure what's hard to ignore."

WHAT THIS MEANS FOR OTHER BRANDS

Southwest's success wasn't about technology alone. It was about reframing what CX measurement is for.

Instead of asking, How are we doing?

They started asking, Where is the customer struggling right now—and what will we do about it today?

That shift—from scorekeeping to real-time signal management—is what sets great companies apart.

Southwest didn't abandon measurement. They evolved it. They activated it. And they made it part of the culture, not just the postmortem.

HOW TO IMPLEMENT A BETTER MEASUREMENT STRATEGY

Moving beyond vanity metrics to measure what matters requires a systematic approach. Here's how companies can recalibrate their measurement strategy:

STEP 1: AUDIT YOUR CURRENT METRICS

Begin by taking a hard look at the metrics you're currently tracking. Are you primarily focusing on traditional measures like NPS, CSAT, and AHT? While these can provide a baseline, ask yourself whether they truly reflect the customer journey. Gather feedback from your frontline teams and your customers themselves to understand what aspects of the experience are most critical to them.

STEP 2: IDENTIFY THE CUSTOMER PAIN POINTS

Analyze your customer interactions to pinpoint where frustration accumulates. Is it during the process of resolving an issue? Do customers have to reach out multiple times for the same problem? Use tools like customer surveys, call recordings, and support ticket analyses to gather qualitative data that can complement your quantitative metrics.

STEP 3: INCORPORATE ACTIONABLE METRICS

Introduce and prioritize metrics that directly relate to customer effort and loyalty. Implement customer effort score (CES) surveys immediately after service interactions to gauge how easy or difficult it was for customers to get their issues resolved. Track repeat contact rates (RCR) to see if problems persist over multiple interactions, and perform churn analysis to understand the underlying reasons why customers leave.

STEP 4: ALIGN METRICS WITH BUSINESS GOALS

Ensure that your chosen metrics align with your broader business objectives. If your goal is to improve customer retention, then focusing on reducing repeat contact rates and customer effort should take precedence. Establish clear targets and tie these metrics to performance incentives for your teams. When everyone in the organization understands that the goal is to reduce friction and build loyalty, it fosters a more customer-centric mindset.

STEP 5: REPORT, ANALYZE, AND ACT

Regularly report on these metrics, not just to show progress but to identify areas needing urgent improvement. Create dashboards that highlight trends over time and correlate them with customer feedback. Use these insights to implement changes—whether that means refining a process, retraining staff, or even overhauling a product feature. Remember, data is only as valuable as the actions it drives. Ensure that insights gleaned from your metrics lead to concrete steps that enhance the customer experience.

STEP 6: FOSTER A CULTURE OF CONTINUOUS IMPROVEMENT

Measurement should not be a one-time project but an ongoing effort. Encourage a culture where every team member, from executives to frontline agents, is committed to continuously improving the customer experience. Regularly review your metrics, celebrate improvements, and learn from setbacks. When everyone in the organization understands that the true measure of success lies in making customers' lives easier, the entire company moves toward that goal.

THE BOTTOM LINE: TRACKING WHAT CREATES LOYALTY, NOT JUST WHAT LOOKS GOOD

At the end of the day, numbers on a report are only valuable if they lead to meaningful change. A high NPS score means little if customers are still struggling with unresolved issues or excessive effort to get their problems fixed. Similarly, a low average handle time isn't a victory if it masks the fact that customers must repeatedly call back for the same issue. The best companies don't just measure performance—they demand actionable insights that drive real improvement.

In a world where customer experience is the ultimate differentiator, measuring the right data is paramount. It's not enough to have impressive charts and graphs in board meetings. What matters is that every metric you track should contribute to creating a smoother, more satisfying customer journey—one that minimizes effort, maximizes resolution, and builds lasting trust.

Ask yourself: Are you measuring what truly matters? Are you tracking the pain points that cause customers to leave, or are you just celebrating numbers that look good on paper? The answer to these questions could very well determine the future success of your brand.

In today's competitive market, where customers have endless choices and high expectations, the companies that measure what matters and act on those insights will be the ones that thrive. They will create experiences that not only meet customer needs but exceed them—turning every interaction into an opportunity to build trust and loyalty.

WHAT GETS MEASURED SHAPES WHAT GETS FIXED

IF YOU WANT A BETTER CUSTOMER EXPERIENCE, START BY ASKING BETTER QUESTIONS

You can't claim to be customer-obsessed and still reward teams for cutting calls short.

You can't talk about loyalty while ignoring effort. And you can't fix what you refuse to measure honestly.

Too many organizations have built their customer experience strategy around metrics that are clean, familiar, and conveniently inoffensive. They're easy to report, easy to track, easy to game—and dangerously easy to misunderstand.

The result? Teams perform for the dashboard, not for the customer. Leaders believe the trendline but miss the exit signs. And the organization starts optimizing for what looks good instead of what is true.

When you measure the right things—when you track friction, effort, emotional tone, and resolution quality—you build a system that doesn't just report experience. It improves it.

Because now your teams can see what's really happening. Now they can connect their work to trust, retention, and impact. Now they can stop playing defense—and start designing better outcomes.

A MESSAGE TO CX LEADERS: MEASUREMENT IS YOUR MANDATE

If you own the customer experience, then you must also own the narrative behind the numbers. Not just the ones that look good in quarterly business reviews—the ones that actually move the needle for your customers. Measurement is not a dashboard. It's a responsibility. It's the discipline of asking harder questions and being brave enough to confront uncomfortable truths, even when they disrupt the story others want to tell.

Most organizations measure what's easy. What's legacy. What keeps people comfortable.

But if you're a true CX leader, your role isn't to keep the boardroom comfortable. It's to keep it honest.

Stop optimizing for what's defendable.

Start optimizing for what's transformational.

It's time to go beyond the basics—because NPS, CSAT, and AHT alone are no longer enough. Not when customers are leaving without saying a word. Not when their frustration hides between the lines of a silent cancellation. Not when your most painful friction points are invisible in your current reporting stack.

Bring forward metrics that expose the real experience:

- Time to recovery, not just time to resolution—because speed means little if the fix doesn't rebuild trust.
- Friction index by journey stage—a quantifiable way to highlight operational drag where it hurts the most.
- Silent churn—those unresolved issues that never escalated but still caused the customer to walk away. That's your early warning signal, and most companies aren't even listening for it.

Push your organization to track the moments between the moments—the digital dead ends, the unreturned follow-ups, the times the customer gave up and solved it themselves.

Don't just analyze contact rates. Analyze dropout points.

Don't just watch the surveys. Watch the silence.

And most importantly: Measure effort like it's a cost center—because it is. The more effort your customers expend, the more value you lose. In repeat contacts. In operational drag. In loyalty erosion. In brand damage. CX is not a service function. It's a risk mitigation engine—and the numbers you track should reflect that.

Your mandate is clear: Defend the customer, not the score.

Be the one in the room who says, "Yes, our metrics are green—but here's why our customers still feel red." Because your job isn't just to measure customer experience. Your job is to ensure it stays grounded in reality, not in reporting theater.

When CX becomes just another report pack, it dies in PowerPoint.

You're here to make sure that doesn't happen.

A MESSAGE TO C-SUITE LEADERS: THIS IS WHAT OWNERSHIP LOOKS LIKE

In every organization, what gets measured gets prioritized—and what gets prioritized reflects what leadership truly values.

If you sit in the C-suite, the metrics your company tracks are more than operational KPIs. They are a cultural statement. They reveal, with brutal clarity, what you care about and what you're willing to ignore.

That's why you cannot outsource metric selection to a dashboard designer or let the scorecard be dictated by inertia.

If your teams are hitting their NPS targets while customer trust is quietly eroding, that's not a data gap—that's a leadership failure.

If your resolution times are improving, but social media complaints are growing louder, that's not just noise—that's your system screaming for help.

You don't need a hundred metrics. You need a handful that matter—and a culture that knows what to do with them.

You need to lead with curiosity, not complacency.

Ask your CX leader, your COO, your Head of Customer Service:

- What metrics do our customers care about that we're not tracking?
- What pain points are our frontline teams dealing with that aren't showing up on our dashboards?
- What does the data say—and what is it not saying that we need to go investigate ourselves?

Then go deeper:

- Are we measuring the things that predict churn, not just report it after the fact?
- Are we holding product, tech, and operations accountable for their role in the experience—or is CX still expected to clean up after them?

- Are we treating customer effort as a cost driver—or as a customer problem someone else owns?

Leadership isn't about reporting green numbers. It's about understanding what's behind them—and acting on what you find.

The best leaders don't just ask for a dashboard. They walk the floor. They listen to call recordings. They read customer complaints with the same urgency as financial audits. Because they understand: How a company treats its customers is one of the most honest reflections of how it operates.

If you're not sure whether your company is measuring the right things, that's your signal to get involved.

Ownership of the experience doesn't mean knowing all the answers. It means asking the right questions—and being willing to act when the answers aren't what you hoped.

This is what ownership looks like.

Key Takeaways

1. Metrics Shape Behavior—So Choose the Right Ones

When you reward speed over resolution, or satisfaction over effort, you build a culture that performs for dashboards instead of customers. What you track becomes what your teams chase—and what they ignore becomes the reason your customers leave.

2. Traditional Metrics Are Incomplete Without Context

NPS, CSAT, and AHT can't tell you where trust is breaking or effort is piling up. To truly understand experience, you must measure friction, failed resolution, silent churn, and emotional recovery—the moments that make-or-break loyalty.

3. Real-Time Insight Creates Real-Time Impact

Dashboards don't fix problems—people do. Companies that listen continuously, route signals intelligently, and empower teams to act with urgency are the ones that build trust faster than it erodes.

CHAPTER 12

Be the Advocate Your Customer Expects You to Be

THE EMPTY CHAIR

It was a product meeting, and the energy in the room was high. A new feature was being reviewed for final approval. Marketing was excited. Engineering had worked through the edge cases. Finance had modeled the revenue lift. Legal had blessed the language.

There was just one problem.

No one had asked what this feature would actually feel like to a customer.

The cancellation path had been deliberately buried in the interface—"standard industry practice," someone offered. The new fee wasn't disclosed until step four. The support script had already been updated...to say it was "part of our evolving product experience."

And no one flinched.

Because in that room—as in so many others—there was no one tasked with asking the uncomfortable question: Would we accept this if we were the customer?

There was no customer advocate at the table. Not a single person who was dedicated to, incented for, or evaluated against representing the customer's experience and emotional response—not after launch, not postmortem, but in the moment where the decision was still being shaped. There was no role, no team, whose full-time job was to challenge, interpret, and defend the customer's perspective before it was too late.

The result wasn't a catastrophic failure. No media crisis. No lawsuits. Just quiet attrition. A wave of customers who clicked, felt tricked, and didn't return.

And by the time the feedback came in, it was already too late. The decision had been made. The emails had been sent. The damage had been done.

This happens every day—not because companies don't care about their customers, but because they forget to represent them when it matters most.

Being the customer advocate isn't just a mindset. It's a mandate. And when no one is structurally responsible—when there's no team whose success is measured by how well the customer is understood, protected, and empowered—that seat in the room stays empty.

And when that chair is empty, customers pay the price.

CUSTOMERS ARE NOT IN THE ROOM— THAT'S THE PROBLEM

ASSUMPTIONS ARE NOT ADVOCACY

Walk into most strategy sessions, budget meetings, or product road mapping workshops, and one thing becomes clear: Decisions are being made by people evaluating what works for the company, not what works for the customer.

It's not malicious. It's operational.

Legal brings risk. Finance brings margin. Product brings velocity. Marketing brings the promise. But the customer? They are often brought in only by proxy—mentioned in passing, represented by a chart, or referenced using survey data that's two quarters old.

No one means to leave the customer out. It's just that their presence isn't institutionalized. They aren't part of the approval path. They're not in the room to raise their hand and say, "This looks great for us... but here's where it's going to frustrate people."

And that's where the breakdown begins.

Because when the customer isn't represented early, their pain will surface later. What starts as a clean internal decision—say, a new subscription model, a tighter return policy, or a redesigned digital flow—can feel like a trap when it lands in the real world. What was defensible in a meeting suddenly feels deceitful to the person on the other end of the screen.

Then come the complaints. The call volume spike. The social media backlash. The drop in retention that shows up two months later, but is almost never tied back to the decision that caused it.

The problem wasn't the customer. It was that no one spoke for them when the stakes were low and the influence was high.

Advocacy delayed is trust denied.

The rooms where decisions are made are full of smart, well-intentioned people. But if no one is trained, empowered, or expected to raise the customer's perspective in real time, then the business is left vulnerable to decisions that make sense internally and feel broken externally.

And in today's market, that kind of misalignment is a liability you can't afford.

CX ISN'T A DEPARTMENT—IT'S A ROLE EVERYONE MUST PLAY

IF YOU TOUCH THE CUSTOMER, YOU OWN THE EXPERIENCE

One of the most common organizational myths is that customer experience is owned by a single team.

That team might report to the COO or CMO. It might oversee surveys, feedback loops, call center performance, or digital journeys. But in reality, no team—no matter how talented—can own the full experience unless the rest of the business understands that they're part of it too.

Because the truth is, most of what defines a customer's experience isn't written in a CX playbook. It's embedded in decisions made upstream—decisions about product timelines, pricing models, policy structures, platform integrations, and communication touchpoints.

Those decisions aren't made by CX teams. They're made by product managers, operations leads, legal advisers, finance partners, and marketing directors. Which means customer experience is not a team. It's a collective outcome. And unless everyone is accountable for their piece of that outcome, the best CX team in the world will be stuck playing cleanup.

What this requires is a mindset shift.

It means product teams start thinking not just about feature velocity, but feature clarity. It means finance begins evaluating not just profitability, but refund friction. It means IT looks at integrations not just through the lens of scalability, but supportability. It means legal considers tone and accessibility, not just coverage.

In the best organizations, this shift is cultural, not procedural. It's not about issuing a memo or rebranding a department. It's about creating a shared standard: If your decision will impact the customer, then it's your job to think like one.

And it's your responsibility to raise your hand when something feels off.

In these companies, people don't wait for a CX team to weigh in. They've internalized the role of advocate. It's embedded in how meetings are run. In how tradeoffs are discussed. In how risk is assessed—not just to the business, but to the relationship the business has with its customers.

They ask questions like: "What does this feel like from the outside?" and "Would this make sense to someone who didn't build it?" Not because it's required, but because it's instinctive.

That's not departmental responsibility. That's cultural ownership.

And it's the only way to ensure that customer experience isn't something you fix later—it's something you design right from the start.

WHAT ADVOCACY ACTUALLY LOOKS LIKE INSIDE THE COMPANY

IT'S NOT ABOUT BEING THE LOUDEST VOICE—IT'S ABOUT BEING THE FIRST TO SEE THE RISK

There's a misconception that advocating for the customer means always siding with them, saying "yes" to every request, or derailing business decisions in the name of empathy. That's not advocacy. That's avoidance.

True customer advocacy is strategic resistance. It's the ability to represent the customer's perspective before the damage is done. It's knowing when to push back, when to reframe a discussion, and when to slow down a decision long enough to consider its downstream impact.

Inside most companies, the advocate's voice is missing not because people don't care—but because they're not sure what advocacy looks like in practice.

So here's what it actually means to advocate:

It means speaking up when a policy is technically correct but emotionally tone-deaf.

It means asking whether a new product feature benefits the customer, or just satisfies an internal milestone.

It means pausing a pricing decision to examine how it will land on the customer's next invoice—not just how it looks in the forecast model.

It means reviewing a communication before it goes live and noticing the line that sounds clever but will feel insulting to someone already frustrated.

These aren't dramatic interventions. They're micro-moves of integrity.

And they matter because they happen at the moment when decisions are still reversible.

Once the email goes out, the damage is public.

Once the policy is enforced, the reputation cost is real.

Once the feature is released, the friction is operational.

Advocacy means stepping in before those moments—when the only cost is discomfort, not churn.

THE ADVOCATE IS THE TRANSLATOR

In many organizations, departments speak their own languages.

Finance talks in margin. Product talks in velocity. Legal talks in liability. Marketing talks in conversion. IT talks in systems and tech stack.

The advocate is the person who hears all of that and asks: "What will the customer hear? What will they feel? How will our customer use this? What does it solve and what will they remember?"

They don't speak for the customer emotionally—they translate the experience into language that each team understands. They help the business see the customer not as an abstraction, but as the recipient of every decision.

They bridge the internal logic with external impact.

And sometimes, they carry the unpopular message: "Just because it's compliant doesn't mean it's fair. Just because it's consistent doesn't mean it's humane."

THE HARDEST PART OF ADVOCACY: BEING WILLING TO DISAGREE

In many rooms, being the customer advocate means being the one person who says, "We might be making a mistake."

It means taking the hit for slowing down a project that's already on the slide deck.

It means questioning assumptions that others have already nodded through.

It means risking your credibility with colleagues in the name of credibility with the customer.

That's not an easy role to play. It requires clarity, courage, and senior-level backing. It requires leaders to reward not just consensus—but conscientious dissent.

Because without it, you create a culture where everyone is aligned, but no one is right.

The most effective advocates aren't loud. They're consistent. They're prepared. And they're trusted—not because they say what leadership wants to hear, but because they've earned the right to be heard when it matters most.

THE COST OF SILENCE—AND THE RISK OF BEING TOO LATE

WHEN YOU DON'T SPEAK UP, THE CUSTOMER ENDS UP PAYING FOR IT

Most poor experiences weren't designed with malice. They were designed in silence.

They weren't created because someone wanted to frustrate customers. They happened because no one questioned the assumptions. Because no one slowed down the sprint. Because no one asked what the downstream impact might be for the people the company claims to serve.

And in that vacuum of dissent—in that absence of advocacy—decisions get made that feel logical inside the building and land like betrayal outside of it.

What starts as a streamlined policy change becomes a surge of complaints.

What looks like an operational improvement becomes a spike in churn.

What was pitched as "industry standard" suddenly reads like a bait-and-switch.

And by the time the data shows up—in refunds, in escalations, in public sentiment—the customer has already paid the price. So have your employees. So has your brand.

Because once you have to explain a decision, the trust is already eroding.

Once you have to apologize for it, you're in recovery mode.

Once it becomes a case study in your competitor's marketing, you've lost more than market share—you've lost the narrative.

THE ECHO CHAMBER OF INTERNAL AGREEMENT

In organizations without a culture of customer advocacy, silence is often mistaken for alignment. There's no pushback, so the assumption is that everyone agrees.

But absence of objection doesn't mean endorsement. It often means people didn't feel safe speaking up. Or they didn't think it was their place. Or they were so used to decisions being made without the customer lens, they stopped expecting anything different.

And so the flawed decision moves forward. No one owns the fallout. And when the customer reacts, the team is surprised—"This isn't what we expected."

Of course it isn't. Because no one asked the one question that would have changed the direction: "What if this actually hurts our customer?"

THE REAL COST ISN'T THE COMPLAINT— IT'S THE CHURN YOU DON'T SEE

When customer advocacy is missing, the damage rarely shows up in one big wave. It shows up in quiet attrition. In once-loyal customers who stop responding. Who don't renew. Who click cancel and never look back.

These customers don't call to complain. They don't take the survey. They don't tell you what went wrong. They simply leave.

And the business chalks it up to market trends, or seasonality, or "normal customer behavior."

But behind that silence is a signal: You stopped listening, so I stopped talking.

And by the time someone realizes what happened, it's too late. The decision that caused it is buried in a meeting no one remembers, made by people who've since moved on.

SILENCE IS NOT A STRATEGY

Waiting to act until complaints come in is not strategy. It's cleanup.

Real advocacy happens upstream. It challenges ideas before they harden into policies. It raises objections before the damage becomes measurable. It prevents the apology email, the PR scramble, the last-minute discount offer to keep a customer from canceling.

Because if the first time your company thinks about the customer is after something goes wrong, you're not doing CX—you're doing damage control.

And eventually, that becomes your brand.

THE COMPANIES GETTING IT RIGHT

WHERE CUSTOMER ADVOCACY ISN'T A DEPARTMENT—IT'S A DISCIPLINE

While many organizations are still trying to define what customer-centricity means in practice, a select few have already built it into the way they operate. Not as a marketing angle or mission statement—but as a cross-functional discipline, embedded into decision-making at every level.

In these companies, the customer doesn't just show up in postmortems. The customer is present in every decision, by design.

WARBY PARKER: CUSTOMER EXPERIENCE AS PRODUCT FEEDBACK LOOP

At Warby Parker, customer advocacy doesn't sit in a corner of the office. It's hardwired into how the business runs.

Support teams don't just answer questions—they gather insights. When multiple customers call about confusing prescription input fields or return instructions that felt unclear, those signals don't disappear into a report. They're flagged, aggregated, and routed directly to product and experience teams.

Every quarter, top friction points from service interactions are reviewed alongside performance metrics—and if the same issue is showing up across multiple customers, it triggers action. Not an apology. A fix.

Warby Parker treats its CX team as an extension of the design process. And that's why their experience feels cohesive—not just convenient.

AMERICAN EXPRESS: EMPOWERED TO SAY YES

American Express is often held up as the gold standard of service—and for good reason. Their agents are empowered to make things right without needing five layers of approval.

But that empowerment isn't just about resolving complaints. It's about preventing customer harm before it happens.

Amex frontline teams are trained to recognize policy friction, emerging confusion, and customer anxiety—and flag those patterns to legal, product, and compliance. If a term is being misunderstood, if a process is consistently resulting in calls, or if a feature is unintentionally excluding people—Amex doesn't wait for the social backlash. They move.

The company trusts its people to act as advocates—and equips them to escalate before it becomes damage control. It's not just a service win. It's a structural advantage.

LEGO: ADVOCATING WITH EMPATHY AT SCALE

LEGO is another brand that understands advocacy isn't just about fixing things. It's about reaffirming relationship.

Their customer service team is empowered not just to issue refunds, but to surprise and delight. To go off-script. To send missing pieces without hassle. To include handwritten notes in replacement orders. Not because it's cost-effective—but because it's relationship-effective.

But more importantly, LEGO listens upstream. They invite feedback from parents, educators, and kids, and that feedback directly influences product design and digital experiences. Their support team is treated as a strategic asset, not an operational cost center.

That mindset—of empowering employees to speak for the customer and act without fear—is what makes LEGO not just beloved, but resilient.

WHAT ALL THESE COMPANIES HAVE IN COMMON

These brands don't delegate advocacy. They institutionalize it.

They don't wait for the CX team to catch the fallout. They build teams, tools, and routines that surface the customer's voice early—and act on it fast.

And they don't treat every customer contact as a cost to manage. They treat it as a moment of truth.

Because in their world, the customer isn't a stakeholder to remember after the fact. They're a presence—always in the room, even when they're not.

THE FIX: GIVE ADVOCACY A SEAT, A VOICE, AND AUTHORITY

CUSTOMER-CENTRIC CULTURES AREN'T DECLARED—THEY'RE DESIGNED

You can't claim to care about the customer and then consistently exclude them from your most important decisions. You can't build loyalty on the back of slogans while policies are written in silos and tradeoffs are made without their perspective in the room.

If advocacy is going to be more than a buzzword, it has to be built into the operating model of the business.

And that starts with structural intent—not just soft skills.

MAKE THE CUSTOMER PART OF EVERY DECISION

First, advocacy must be positioned as a standing voice in decision-making—not an occasional check-in or afterthought.

When product is building a new journey, the customer's effort must be considered alongside engineering feasibility. When pricing is being reviewed, the customer's perceived fairness must sit next to projected margin. When legal is writing a policy, someone has to ask, "What will this feel like when it's enforced?"

That doesn't mean giving customers a literal vote. It means assigning someone—ideally, multiple people—the responsibility to speak on their behalf when no one else will.

If every meeting includes legal, finance, product, and engineering—but not CX, operations, or service—then you're building in risk by design.

EMPOWER PEOPLE TO SPEAK FOR THE CUSTOMER— EVEN WHEN IT'S UNCOMFORTABLE

Too many organizations say they value the customer but punish the people who speak up when it matters most.

True advocacy can't live in a culture where dissent is discouraged. It can't thrive in an environment where timelines are sacred, but trust is expendable. And it certainly can't take hold if customer defenders are told to stay in their lane.

The best leaders reward people who say, "This might not land well." They listen when someone says, "I know this meets the business case—but it breaks the customer experience." They pause before launch to make sure the journey works not just for the brand, but for the person at the other end of the screen, phone, or checkout.

That's not idealism. That's good business.

BUILD ADVOCACY INTO THE OPERATING MODEL

Advocacy must be both cultural and procedural. That means:

- Including CX leaders in roadmap prioritization
- Making customer impact a required dimension in executive decision frameworks
- Reviewing key customer insights alongside financials in boardroom discussions
- Establishing escalation pathways for customer risk before something goes live

When these structures are absent, advocacy becomes reactive—a tool used after the backlash, instead of before the decision.

When they're present, advocacy becomes proactive. And that's where transformation happens.

THIS IS A LEADERSHIP IMPERATIVE

Companies don't accidentally become customer centric. They architect for it.

They make sure someone in the room has the customer's perspective—not in theory, but in detail. They build feedback into every cycle. They don't just empower advocates—they expect them.

And they model it from the top.

Because if the CEO, the CFO, the COO, and the CMO aren't thinking about what this decision feels like to the people they claim to serve, then it doesn't matter how friendly your app is. The relationship is already at risk.

You don't need a customer advocacy committee.

You need leaders who refuse to sign off on a decision until someone has asked—"Would I accept this experience if I were on the other side?"

That's not a checklist. That's a standard.

And it's one that separates the companies customers tolerate from the ones they trust.

THE CUSTOMER SHOULD NEVER BE THE LAST TO KNOW

BY THE TIME THEY FEEL IT, IT'S ALREADY TOO LATE

If you've ever seen a customer response that blindsided your team—a surge of cancellations, a backlash to a policy change, a flood of frustrated calls over something that "shouldn't have been a big deal"—then you already know the truth:

The customer was left out of the room.

Someone signed off. Someone built the thing. Someone sent the message. But no one said, "Hold on—how does this actually feel when you're on the other side?"

By the time the complaints hit, the moment to act has already passed. The experience was designed. The systems were shipped. The harm was done. And all that's left to manage is the reaction—the reviews, the escalations, the churn.

This is how brands erode themselves: not through dramatic failures, but through small, compounding decisions that feel good inside the business and feel terrible outside of it.

Because when no one speaks for the customer, the business ends up speaking at them—and then wondering why they're no longer listening.

ADVOCACY IS PREVENTION, NOT APOLOGY

A great customer advocate doesn't wait for the complaint. They anticipate it. They sense when a decision is about to go sideways—not because they're psychic, but because they've learned to hear what's missing from the conversation.

They know that risk doesn't always show up in a spreadsheet.

That trust isn't always captured by a survey.

That just because a feature meets spec doesn't mean it earns loyalty.

Advocates speak up when it would be easier to stay quiet.

They slow the process when it would be more comfortable to keep moving.

And they do it not to protect the company from the customer—but to protect the relationship from the company's blind spots.

IF YOU WAIT FOR THE COMPLAINT, YOU'VE ALREADY LOST THE MOMENT

Customers don't churn because of one bad experience. They churn because they no longer believe anyone inside the company is paying attention. They don't need everything to be perfect—but they need someone to notice when it isn't. Someone to say, "This isn't just a ticket. It's a moment."

And if that person doesn't exist—if the advocate never shows up—then the customer stops believing you're building anything for them at all.

So they stop showing up too.

BE THE ONE WHO DOESN'T LET IT SLIDE

This isn't just about CX teams. It's about product leaders, policy writers, compliance reviewers, marketing strategists, and finance planners. It's about executives and entry-level employees alike.

Advocacy isn't about hierarchy. It's about integrity.

It's the willingness to ask hard questions. To challenge the easy answer. To slow down something that might hit a revenue goal—but break a relationship.

If your company claims to be customer-led, this is where that promise is tested: not in the onboarding deck or the brand campaign, but in the moment someone quietly suggests a shortcut—and you say, "No, that's not who we are."

THE CUSTOMER DESERVES MORE THAN A FIX—THEY DESERVE A VOICE

You can't keep asking customers for their feedback if you're not willing to advocate for them when it counts. You can't build trust if you only listen after the fact.

Advocacy means the customer is never the last to know.

They're considered. They're protected. They're anticipated.

And that only happens when someone in the room is willing to carry their voice, even when it's inconvenient.

That someone is you.

Key Takeaways

1. Advocacy Isn't a department—It's a Discipline

Every function impacts the customer. If you touch the product, policy, platform, or process, then you own a piece of the experience. Advocacy starts when people stop saying, "That's not my job," and start asking, "How will this land with the customer?"

2. Silence Is Where Bad Decisions Take Root

When no one speaks for the customer in the room, flawed logic passes as strategy. The result? Quiet attrition, noisy complaints, and costly recoveries. Advocacy is what prevents churn before it's visible.

3. Leadership Means Asking the Hard Questions First

The best leaders don't just sign off. They interrogate decisions. They require someone to answer, "Would we accept this if we were on the receiving end?" Advocacy isn't just empathy—it's accountability.

CHAPTER 13

C-Suite—It's Your Problem to Fix

WHAT IF THE CUSTOMER GOT A SEAT AT YOUR QUARTERLY BUSINESS REVIEW—OR YOUR INVESTOR DAY? IT'S THE PERFORMANCE REVIEW NO ONE WANTS TO HAVE.

Imagine your next QBR starts a little differently.

The room is filled with the usual players. Finance, marketing, product, operations—everyone ready to walk through the numbers. Revenue is steady. Retention looks "manageable." Digital projects are on track. The slide deck is tight. The room is confident.

And then, someone walks in who wasn't on the invite list:

A customer.

Not a made-up persona. Not a quote pulled from a survey. A real customer—the kind who used to be loyal, who tried to engage, who gave feedback until they finally gave up.

They sit down and quietly place a stack of evidence on the table. Screenshots of confusing policies. Email threads that went nowhere. An invoice that doesn't match the promise on your home page. They pull out the chatbot transcript, the support ticket, the long-forgotten NPS survey they answered with a three and never heard back from.

They're not here to vent.

They're here to ask questions.

The same way your investors ask questions.

The same way analysts press you on margins and capital efficiency.

Except this time, the questions are about loyalty, not leverage.

They ask, "Who reviewed the new return policy before it went live?"

"Why does the app make me repeat my issue every time I open a chat?"

"Who decided I should wait six weeks for a refund but be charged in six seconds?"

And then they ask the question that hits hardest:

"You talk about being customer-obsessed...when was the last time someone here actually acted like it?"

Now imagine that same customer is invited to your Investor Day.

They sit beside your institutional shareholders.

They listen to the leadership team lay out the strategy.

They hear about EBITDA growth, digital innovation, and net revenue retention.

Then they raise their hand and ask, "If I'm the source of all that value... why do I feel like I was never part of the conversation?"

It's uncomfortable. Because it's real.

And it exposes the gap—not just between the promise and the experience, but between the accountability you expect from your teams and the accountability your customers expect from you.

Your investors get direct access.

They get Q&A.

They get visibility.

What would happen if your customers got the same?

If they had a seat at the table when decisions were made.

If they were there when tradeoffs were justified.

If they heard firsthand how their experience was deprioritized in favor of "what the model can absorb."

This is the performance review no executive ever schedules—but every customer conducts.

And it happens every day, in silence.

In cancellations. In negative word of mouth. In quietly shrinking loyalty.

You may never hear it in your boardroom.

But your customers are watching—and deciding.

And if no one in the C-suite is asking their questions for them,

don't be surprised when they stop waiting for answers.

YOU SAY THE RIGHT THINGS—BUT THE CUSTOMER DOESN'T SEE IT

TRUST ISN'T BUILT IN SLOGANS—IT'S BUILT IN SYSTEMS

Let's be clear: Most executive teams believe they care about the customer.

They say the right things. They fund customer experience programs. They speak about empathy in town halls. "The customer is at the center of everything we do" is printed on decks, hung on walls, and recited in interviews.

But when the customer interacts with the company—when they actually need help, clarity, flexibility, or fairness—they're met with something else entirely.

They encounter friction. They encounter indifference. They encounter rigid processes and disconnected channels. And most importantly, they encounter people who want to help—but can't. Because the system wasn't designed for resolution. It was designed for containment.

And that's when the disconnect is exposed.

The customer hears your mission—and experiences something that undermines it.

They see your ads—and get a refund policy that feels like a trap.

They hear your promises—and end up repeating their story to a third agent.

It's not the words that fail you.

It's the fact that nothing in the organization is designed to make those words real.

THE CUSTOMER HAS LEARNED TO STOP LISTENING

Today's customer is savvy. They've been through too many bait-and-switches. They've read too many "We care about your feedback" emails that lead nowhere. They've seen "Your call is important to us" messages play on hold loops that last forty-five minutes.

So when they hear a CEO say, "We put the customer first," they don't believe it because it sounds wrong.

They don't believe it because they can't find any evidence of it when it matters.

The customer doesn't experience strategy. They experience outcomes.

They don't experience your intent. They experience your infrastructure.

And if those things are out of sync with your messaging, they don't give you grace—they give you distance.

You may win them with vision.

But you lose them in execution.

THE GAP BETWEEN TALK AND ACTION IS A LEADERSHIP PROBLEM

It's not your CX team that's failing.

It's your structure.

It's your decision hierarchy.

It's the prioritization frameworks that allow a broken journey to persist quarter after quarter while the company celebrates brand campaigns that have nothing to do with operational truth.

When leadership doesn't connect the dots between promise and experience, it's not just a missed opportunity. It's a breach of trust.

Because every time the customer hears your words but feels your absence, they draw the same conclusion:

"They know how to say the right thing—they just don't care enough to fix the right thing."

CX IS TREATED LIKE A TREND—UNTIL IT'S A CRISIS

IT'S A TALKING POINT WHEN IT SHOULD BE AN OPERATING MODEL

Customer experience isn't a new idea. It's been talked about at conferences, headlined in earnings calls, and featured in more slide decks than most C-suite leaders can count.

But inside many companies, CX still lives on the surface—more slogan than strategy. It's something to champion in good times, showcase during transformations, and spotlight in brand narratives. But as soon as pressure hits—as soon as budgets tighten or product launches slip—it becomes one of the first things deprioritized.

That's because many executive teams still treat CX like a trend. Something to focus on this quarter. Something to sponsor. Something to feature on the home page when sentiment looks soft.

But customer experience isn't a campaign.

It's not a messaging layer.

It's not a differentiator you can toggle on and off.

It's the system that holds every other promise accountable.

When you treat it like a trend, you build it for optics.

When you treat it like a discipline, you build it for resilience.

CX DOESN'T MATTER—UNTIL IT SUDDENLY DOES

Too often, CX becomes urgent only when it becomes a problem.

- When churn jumps ten points.
- When social backlash goes viral.
- When a competitor uses your customer pain points as a marketing hook.
- When customers flee despite pricing discounts and loyalty perks.

Then—and only then—do executives lean in. They call emergency meetings. They ask why no one raised the red flags. They demand dashboards, diagnostics, and immediate improvements.

But by the time it shows up in churn, the trust has already been broken.

By the time it shows up in brand reputation, the erosion has already taken hold.

By the time it shows up in revenue, it's already too expensive to ignore.

This isn't reaction. It's reactivity.

And it reveals what's always been true: CX wasn't part of the operating model. It was part of the marketing language.

REAL CX STRATEGY DOESN'T PANIC. IT PREPARES.

The most customer-committed companies don't wait for backlash to act. They bake experience into every layer of the business:

- In how they design product feedback loops
- In how they tie CX metrics to performance reviews
- In how they fund resolution capability, not just response capability
- In how they ensure every decision—from pricing to policy—is measured against a customer trust threshold

That's what separates leadership teams that say, "CX is one of our values," from the ones who build their business around delivering it.

Customer experience isn't a seasonal theme.

It's the scoreboard of how serious you are about delivering what you promised.

And the customers always know whether you're keeping score.

WHAT YOU'RE MISSING AS A LEADERSHIP TEAM

IT'S NOT WHAT YOU SEE THAT'S HURTING YOU—IT'S WHAT YOU'VE DECIDED NOT TO LOOK AT

Many executive teams genuinely believe they're customer focused.

They fund digital tools. They run surveys. They assign net promoter score (NPS) targets. They host customer panels and send personalized thank-you emails to high-value clients. But for all the activity, most are missing the one thing that matters most:

What does the customer actually feel?

Not what they say on a five-point survey.

Not what shows up in a dashboard summary.

Not what the quarterly sentiment tracker says.

What they feel—in the moment they try to get help, solve a problem, or make sense of a policy you approved.

And the reason that truth stays hidden? Because no one at the leadership table is getting close enough to experience it themselves.

YOU'VE GOT METRICS—BUT YOU'RE MISSING MEANING

It's easy to feel informed when you've got numbers. NPS. CSAT. FCR. AHT. Even real-time analytics from your CRM or customer engagement platforms.

But metrics don't equal truth. They're snapshots. Lagging signals. Often too sanitized to provoke real accountability. They make it easy to assume things are fine—especially if no one is bringing the human reality behind them into the room.

What's missing is the voice of the front line—the agent who handled the same unresolved billing issue fourteen times this week. The operations lead who's still waiting for someone to fix the policy customers keep getting caught in. The customer who didn't fill out your survey because they already decided they're not coming back.

You don't see those things on your dashboards.

But your CX team does.

And your customers definitely do.

THE ORG CHART IS SENDING THE WRONG SIGNAL

In many companies, the person responsible for customer experience reports two or three levels down. Buried in marketing. Tucked under operations. Caught between functions. No clear seat at the decision-making table. No direct line to the people who control priorities, investment, or accountability.

That structure sends a message—to the company, and to the customer.

It says CX is something we manage, not something we lead.

It says experience is reactive, not strategic.

It says we care about customers—but not enough to give them a voice at the table where tradeoffs are made.

If the person responsible for customer trust doesn't have real power, then every other department has permission to make decisions that affect customers without ever consulting the people who understand them best.

That's not just a structure problem. That's a leadership failure.

YOU'VE DESIGNED FOR THE COMPANY— NOT FOR THE CUSTOMER

Too many C-suites are still asking, "How do we make this easier for us?"

Easier to fulfill.

Easier to standardize.

Easier to defend.

And in doing so, they've unintentionally made things harder for the customer—more confusing, more effortful, more exhausting.

What starts as an internal win becomes an external pain point.

What feels like efficiency becomes a loyalty leak.

And the scariest part is: No one is connecting those dots. Because the people making the decisions are shielded from the experience they've created.

This is what you're missing.

And this is what the customer is quietly punishing.

CX NEEDS TO REPORT TO THE
C-SUITE—AND HERE'S WHY

IF CUSTOMER EXPERIENCE DOESN'T HAVE
POWER, IT DOESN'T HAVE A CHANCE

You can't say the customer is your top priority—and then place the person responsible for their experience two or three levels away from any real power.

You can't claim to be customer-obsessed and then make them compete with ad spend, sales enablement, or infrastructure upgrades just to get a seat at the table.

If CX isn't reporting directly to the C-suite, it's not leading the business. It's reacting to it.

And that's why so many brands sound like they care about the customer—but don't operate like they do.

CX doesn't have a competing priority. Let me say that again, CX doesn't have a competing priority. That's exactly why it needs its own seat.

Let's be clear: Every function in your organization has a defined objective.

- Marketing's priority is brand visibility and campaign performance.
- Sales is focused on growth, pipelines, and quotas.
- Technology is managing uptime, integrations, and product roadmaps.
- Finance is watching cost control and margin efficiency.

None of these are wrong. They're necessary. But none of them are explicitly designed to represent the experience of the customer—especially not when that experience conflicts with internal goals.

This is where CX gets lost.

When you place customer experience under marketing, it becomes a branding tool.

Under operations, it becomes a cost-center efficiency play.

Under product, it becomes a feature adoption metric.

Under technology, it becomes a ticket log.

Under sales, it becomes a post-close apology team.

In each of those scenarios, customer experience is forced to compete for attention, budget, and legitimacy. It's fighting uphill—constantly deprioritized in favor of "harder" metrics with more political capital behind them.

That's why it needs its own line to the top.

CX is the only function whose job is to make sure the customer doesn't pay the price for everyone else meeting their goals.

WHAT YOU'RE REALLY SAYING WITH YOUR ORG CHART

The reporting structure tells the truth—even if the mission statement doesn't.

If the person accountable for the customer's experience doesn't report to the CEO, COO, or someone with direct enterprise authority, here's what it signals:

- "The customer is important… but not as important as operations."
- "We want great experiences… but only if they don't interfere with marketing campaigns."
- "We care about retention… but not enough to fund it unless there's a crisis."

That structure teaches the rest of the organization exactly how to treat CX: as something to mention, not something to own.

STRUCTURAL POWER CHANGES STRATEGIC OUTCOMES

When CX has a direct line to the C-suite, everything changes.

Now, decisions are filtered through the lens of trust.

Now, customer signals are used to prevent issues—not just apologize for them.

Now, someone at the table is authorized to say: "We can't launch this until it makes sense to the people who will actually use it."

This isn't about titles or politics. It's about aligning influence with accountability.

If CX owns the customer, then CX needs the authority to protect them—even when that means slowing things down, saying no, or questioning a roadmap that looks great on a slide but feels broken in real life.

THE C-SUITE MUST CHOOSE: LIP SERVICE OR LEADERSHIP

Customer experience doesn't need sponsorship. It needs governance.

It doesn't need permission. It needs priority.

And that only happens when it has the structural standing to advocate without fear, escalate without resistance, and lead without having to prove—quarter after quarter—that the customer matters.

Give it the reporting line it deserves.

And watch the entire company start acting like the customer matters.

Not just in sentiment.

But in structure.

THE QUESTIONS YOU'RE NOT ASKING—BUT SHOULD BE

YOU'RE MEASURING PERFORMANCE. BUT ARE YOU MEASURING REGRET?

Executives pride themselves on asking sharp questions. They challenge growth assumptions, poke holes in financial forecasts, and demand rigor around operational readiness. But when it comes to customer experience, that same edge often goes dull.

Too many C-suites ask polite questions. Safe questions. Questions designed to validate the dashboard instead of interrogating the experience.

"What's our NPS this quarter?"

"Are we closing tickets fast enough?"

"Is customer satisfaction holding steady?"

"Have we rolled out the new feedback tool?"

These are comfortable questions.

They're also shallow.

They don't reveal the truth.

They don't show you what's at risk.

And they certainly don't tell you what the customer is trying to say between the metrics.

Because while you're asking about performance, your customer is quietly deciding whether to stay—or leave.

THE QUESTIONS THAT ACTUALLY SURFACE RISK

If you want to lead a company customers trust, you have to ask questions that make people pause. That force them to tell the real story. That challenge them to go deeper than the survey data or the contact center stats.

You need to ask:

"Where are we unintentionally eroding trust right now?"

This question assumes that even well-meaning decisions carry risk. It invites teams to bring forward concerns they've been sitting on. It shifts the posture from defensiveness to curiosity. You're not looking for fault. You're looking for early signs of fatigue, friction, or fear—before they become viral complaints or measurable churn.

"What processes or policies do we keep defending—even though we know they frustrate customers?"

Every company has these. The "it's always been this way" systems. The refund rules no one likes but legal insists on. The policy language that doesn't make sense but has survived three redesigns. This question forces a reckoning with legacy decisions that are actively doing damage. It gives your teams permission to challenge what was once untouchable.

"Where have we built something that serves the company more than it serves the customer?"

This isn't a trick question—it's a blueprint for reform. It helps expose pricing models that are too complex, service channels that are built to deflect rather than resolve, or digital journeys that prioritize conversion over clarity. And it uncovers where short-term efficiency is silently draining long-term loyalty.

"What pain have we normalized because it doesn't show up in a chart?"

Just because something isn't measured doesn't mean it's not hurting you. This is how you surface friction in quiet places—the poor password reset experience, the lack of human escalation, the absence of confirmation emails that leave customers anxious. These microfailures don't always escalate—but they accumulate.

"What stories are we not hearing—and why?"

When customers go silent, that's not satisfaction. It's disengagement. This question reframes the absence of complaints as a possible warning sign. It shifts focus from loud signals (like bad reviews or escalations) to the subtle indicators of withdrawal—disengagement, opt-outs, drop-offs, hesitation.

WHY THESE QUESTIONS MATTER

These questions aren't about blame—they're about exposure.

They expose friction hiding in process.

They expose risk buried in legacy systems.

They expose decay masked by positive metrics.

And most importantly, they expose the gap between what the business sees and what the customer feels.

That gap is where most brand damage begins.

That gap is where loyalty starts to evaporate.

And that gap is where executive leadership needs to step in—not just to approve funding, but to drive a deeper kind of accountability.

WHAT CHANGES WHEN YOU ASK BETTER QUESTIONS

When the C-suite starts asking these questions consistently and publicly, three things happen:

- The truth surfaces faster.

  People stop editing the story. They bring the real feedback—even when it's uncomfortable—because they know it's safe to tell the truth. Middle managers stop oversanitizing. CX teams stop burying edge cases. And the organization starts solving actual problems instead of chasing scores.

- The company reorients around the customer.

  These questions force every department to see how their work affects trust. Suddenly, finance is talking about refund friction. Product is asking about effort. Legal is reviewing how a policy feels, not just whether it protects. That's when you know the culture is shifting—when functions start self-regulating based on the customer impact, not just internal incentives.

- You stop getting surprised.

  There's no more scrambling to explain a churn spike or defend a social backlash. You already knew it was coming. Because someone asked the question no one else wanted to—and someone else was ready with the answer.

LEADERSHIP ISN'T IN THE ANSWERS—IT'S IN THE QUESTIONS

If you're only asking about CX performance, you'll get performance.

But if you ask about trust, clarity, fairness, and regret—you'll get insight.

Not the kind that flatters the strategy.

The kind that strengthens it.

Because the goal isn't to find a flaw and assign blame.

It's to find the friction and remove it—before the customer decides for you.

WALK THE PROPERTY—OR STOP PRETENDING YOU'RE CUSTOMER-CENTRIC

YOU CAN'T FIX WHAT YOU'VE NEVER EXPERIENCED

There's a phrase that shows up often in executive meetings: "That's not a big deal."

It's said in response to a complaint. A customer story. An edge case.

But what's considered "not a big deal" inside the boardroom often feels like a breaking point to the customer on the other end.

Why the disconnect?

Because too many executives are making decisions about experiences they've never actually lived through.

They're managing dashboards, not journeys.

They're reviewing metrics, not moments.

They're approving customer-facing policies they've never had to follow.

And as a result, the company builds systems that look efficient from the inside—and feel exhausting from the outside.

WHEN'S THE LAST TIME YOU TRIED TO BE A CUSTOMER?

Not in theory. Not by reading a survey.

But for real.

Have you tried navigating your website from a mobile device on spotty Wi-Fi?

Have you attempted to cancel a subscription through the same channel it was purchased?

Have you listened to a full support call—from the customer's first prompt to the final closeout?

Have you followed a billing dispute through to resolution, with no executive shortcuts?

If the answer is no—or if it's been a while—then you're operating on assumption.

And assumption is what leads to erosion.

You don't know how bad the return experience is until you've tried it.

You don't know how degrading the chatbot flow feels until you've been stuck in it.

You don't know how broken a promise looks until you've read the marketing line and then hit the policy page.

These are not abstract problems. They are the daily proof points—or contradictions—of your brand.

"WALKING THE PROPERTY" ISN'T SYMBOLIC—IT'S STRATEGIC

When hotel GMs walk their property, they don't just wave at the staff and glance at the lobby. They check the hallway lighting. They sit in the guest chairs. They flush the toilets. They make sure that what was promised is actually being delivered—and if not, they take accountability for fixing it.

C-suite leaders must do the same.

Walk the property. Not ceremonially—operationally.

Use the product. Submit the support ticket. Attempt the refund. Experience the password reset, the queue time, the fine print.

You'll notice things your metrics don't capture.

You'll feel things your dashboards can't report.

And you'll remember what it's like to be the customer—not just talk about them.

That insight? It's irreplaceable.

Because once you've felt the experience yourself, you'll stop approving decisions that make someone else endure what you wouldn't.

Because leadership doesn't sit above the experience.

It sits inside it.

FINAL MESSAGE: IT'S NOT YOUR CX TEAM THAT'S FAILING. IT'S YOU.

STOP DELEGATING THE CUSTOMER. START LEADING FOR THEM.

If the experience is broken, it's not because your CX team isn't doing their job.

It's because you've positioned them in the org as if their job is small.

You've treated them like a necessary function—there to answer phones, deflect issues, and make customers feel "heard" after something goes wrong.

But that's not who they are.

Your CX team is the most underleveraged strategic asset in the company.

They are the only team that talks to customers every day.

They see the patterns. They hear the emotion. They know where trust is breaking—in real time.

And yet, they're often excluded from product decisions, buried under operations, underfunded in the name of efficiency, and left to clean up what could have been prevented.

This isn't just organizational neglect.

It's a leadership failure.

START SHOWING YOUR COMPANY WHO THE CUSTOMER ADVOCATE REALLY IS

It's time to change the way your business sees CX—and the way you, as a leader, talk about them.

Stop saying they "own the customer" and then undercutting their influence.

Stop assigning them postmortem work without giving them access to upstream decisions.

Stop treating them like a department that "handles complaints," and start recognizing them as the only team brave enough to speak for the customer when no one else will.

They're not there to manage sentiment.

They're there to protect the relationship.

And if you don't elevate that role—visibly, structurally, and financially—you're sending a message to your entire company that what they do doesn't matter.

So don't just say the words. Prove it.

Put your CX leaders at the table.

Give them authority, not just accountability.

Tell your colleagues and teams exactly why CX has a voice in every room: because someone needs to represent the customer when there's still time to get it right.

THE DISCONNECT ISN'T INVISIBLE—IT'S JUST UNCHALLENGED

Your customers can feel it.

They know when your brand says one thing and delivers another.

They know when "your call is important to us" is just a script.

They know when the agent on the line is trying their best—but the system behind them is broken.

And if your leadership team isn't listening to those signals, you're not leading.

You're managing sentiment while ignoring substance.

This is the moment to stop hiding behind KPIs and call center metrics.

This is where you stop viewing CX as a team that "answers to the customer," and start realizing they're the ones who answer for the customer—inside your company.

And they can't do that without your full, public, structural support.

YOU HOLD THE POWER—USE IT

You control the org chart.

You approve the funding.

You set the tone for how the business views customer experience.

So if the experience still feels inconsistent, transactional, or fragile—the issue isn't the people working in CX.

It's that they haven't been positioned to lead.

That's on you.

You don't need another customer journey map.

You need the courage to walk into your next leadership meeting and say:

"If we're serious about the customer, then CX doesn't answer to marketing, to ops, or to tech. It answers to me."

Because this is where you stop delegating empathy.

This is where you stop assigning customer impact to a department.

This is where you start leading like it actually matters.

Key Takeaways

1. Customer Experience Is Not a Department—It's a Strategic Discipline That Must Report to the Top

If your CX team is buried under marketing, operations, or tech, you've reduced them to support staff. If you want real impact, CX must report directly to the C-suite—with authority, budget, and the power to say, "This hurts the customer," and be heard.

2. Stop Delegating Empathy and Start Leading It

Your CX team is not just answering phones. They're advocating for your customers in a system that doesn't always make that easy. It's your job to champion them—not just with words, but with structure. Visibility is not enough. Give them a seat and a voice.

3. If You're Not Asking the Right Questions, You're Building the Wrong Company

Dashboards won't show you where trust is leaking. Loyalty lives in the moments no one is tracking. Start asking: Where are we eroding trust? What are we normalizing that frustrates customers? And who's in the room speaking on their behalf before it's too late?

CHAPTER 14

Final Thoughts

After decades in this industry—across global brands, industries, and leadership teams—one truth has stayed painfully consistent: We're still getting the basics wrong.

Not because leaders don't care. Not because teams aren't working hard. And certainly not because customers are asking for too much.

We're getting the basics wrong because modern business is louder, faster, and more complex than it has ever been. Decisions are made in hours, not weeks. Priorities shift in real time. Teams are being asked to do more with less, while navigating cross-functional tension, digital transformation, and AI disruption—all at once.

In that kind of environment, it's easy to miss the fundamentals, create the gaps.

Not out of neglect—but out of velocity.

So this isn't a critique. It's a call to recenter.

Because when everything is moving faster, the basics matter more, not less.

Empathy. Clarity. Resolution. Consistency.

These are not soft skills. They are operational differentiators.

And right now, too many companies are sprinting past the very things that would make them unshakable.

You can launch new features.

You can automate journeys.

You can modernize your channels.

But if your customer still feels ignored when something breaks—you haven't evolved. You've just scaled the friction.

This is the gap.

And it's more than an experience problem—it's a leadership one.

Because in a competitive marketplace, the gap between what you say and what you deliver isn't just frustrating. It's fatal. Customers don't leave because you made a mistake. They leave because no one stepped up to fix it when they did.

And your competitor? They're building to make that moment effortless.

That's the difference.

IT STARTS WITH RESPECT—AND ENDS WITH ACCOUNTABILITY

Let's start with something simple: Stop thinking of your customer experience team as the group that answers the phones.

They are not "just" support. They are your early warning system, your feedback loop, and your brand recovery engine—often all in the same day. They are closer to your customers than anyone else in your organization.

But too often, they're left fighting fires without the tools, the data, or the authority to fix what's broken upstream.

If you want a better customer experience, start by showing your team that what they do matters. Give them visibility across the business. Give them access to the conversations where customer-impacting decisions are made. And most of all, give them permission to challenge what no longer serves the customer—even if it means questioning what has always been done.

That's not disloyalty. That's leadership.

WALK THE PROPERTY—AND THEN FIX THE FOUNDATION

As I've said throughout this book, "walking the property" isn't just a metaphor. It's a leadership habit. It's the practice of stepping into your customer's shoes—using your own service channels, testing your own tools, navigating your own processes—not as an executive, but as a user.

Because if you haven't experienced what it feels like to cancel your product, request a refund, get stuck in a policy loop, or escalate a ticket—then you are not qualified to approve the current experience.

And what you'll often discover is that it's not one big failure. It's a thousand small ones. Systems that weren't designed to talk to each other. Policies that made sense on paper but feel punishing in practice. Messaging that sounds great in marketing but lands hollow in support.

Fixing this doesn't start with slogans. It starts with structure.

TECHNOLOGY SHOULD BE A TOOL—NOT A BARRIER

Today, you have more tools than ever to close the gap—to make it easier for customers to get what they need, and for your teams to deliver it with confidence.

- You have real-time feedback platforms that surface moments of friction as they happen.
- You have customer journey analytics that show you where the experience breaks down.
- You have AI-powered assistants that can automate routine work and free up your teams to focus on moments that matter.

But none of these tools will matter if they're not used with intention.

Technology should enable empathy, not replace it.

It should empower your teams, not burden them.

It should help you know your customer better—not just track them.

The best companies are using AI not to cut corners, but to create clarity. They're using it to summarize complex cases, flag sentiment trends, and surface high-risk churn signals before the customer leaves. They're using it to do the right thing—faster.

That's what it means to use tools wisely: not to scale efficiency at the expense of humanity, but to scale humanity through smarter, more responsive systems.

EDUCATE YOUR TEAMS. TRUST YOUR TEAMS.

If you want to be known as a company that gets customer experience right, then your frontline teams can't be the last to know about what matters.

Train them—not just in policy, but in purpose.

Teach them not just how to close tickets, but how to build trust.

Give them the tools to understand customer sentiment, resolve issues across channels, and escalate without fear of repercussion.

But above all, trust them. Listen to them. Trust them to make judgment calls. Trust them to challenge a broken process. Trust them to know when the rule needs to be flexed for the sake of the relationship.

Because the moment your employees believe they're allowed to do the right thing—and equipped to do it—that's the moment your customer starts to believe in your brand again.

STOP TREATING CX LIKE A TALKING POINT

Customer experience is not your brand voice.

It's not your net promoter score.

It's not the language in your welcome email.

It's what happens when your system is stressed.

It's what's left when the customer has to fight to be understood.

It's what they feel when no one calls them back—and when no one is accountable for making it right.

This isn't about one department.

This is about how your company shows up when it matters.

And if you're still treating CX like a campaign—something to rebrand, to score, to perform—you're not leading. You're posturing.

Your customers are smarter than that. So are your teams.

THIS IS THE MOMENT TO GET IT RIGHT

There has never been a better time—or a bigger imperative—to build companies that get this right. Companies that know their customers, honor their time, respect their intelligence, and invest in the systems that make it easier to stay than to leave.

This is the next competitive advantage.

It's not product alone. It's not price. It's the experience.

Because experiences don't just influence preference—they create belief.

So as you step into your next leadership meeting, here's the question to carry with you:

"Are we building something we'd be proud to offer to someone we love?"

If the answer is yes—then keep going.

If the answer is no—then stop.

Fix it. Walk the property. Listen to your customer. Ask the hard questions. Empower your teams. Use the tools.

Lead like it matters.

Because it does.

And your customers are watching.

ACKNOWLEDGMENTS

To the extraordinary community of colleagues, mentors, partners, and customers who have been part of this journey—thank you.

For more than thirty years, I've had the privilege of working alongside some of the brightest, boldest, and most passionate people in this industry. You've challenged me, taught me, trusted me, and above all, inspired me.

To my teams—past and present—you have been the heartbeat of this work. You showed up every day with conviction, integrity, and an unwavering commitment to do right by the customer. You made the mission real.

To my mentors and peers, thank you for pushing me further than I thought possible—for asking hard questions, sharing wisdom generously, and reminding me that leadership is about listening as much as leading.

To the global customer experience community: I remain deeply grateful to be part of this movement. You are the reason I continue to speak, write, and advocate—for better systems, smarter technology, and a seat at the decision-making table for the customer.

This work is far from done.

Our industry has never mattered more. My mission is simple: to educate, inspire, and elevate the work we all do—so that customers aren't an afterthought, but a guiding voice.

This journey has given me far more than professional milestones. It's given me lifelong friendships, hard-earned lessons, and a deep belief that our work—done right—can change not just companies, but lives.

Thank you for walking this road with me. Here's to what we've built—and what we will build next.

Lance

REFERENCES & RESOURCES

The insights, data, and frameworks in this book are drawn from a combination of frontline leadership experience, customer feedback analysis, and respected industry research. The following sources were referenced throughout the chapters to ground the narrative in real-world evidence and trusted benchmarks.

SUPPORTING RESEARCH AND SOURCES USED THROUGHOUT THIS BOOK

INDUSTRY RESEARCH & REPORTS

- Accenture. (2023). Global Consumer Pulse Survey: The Human Paradox. Accenture Interactive.
- Deloitte Digital & MIT Sloan Management Review. (2022). Customer Experience: Is It the New Competitive Advantage?
- Forrester Research. (2023). Predictions 2024: Customer Experience Strategy.
- Gartner. (2023). Top Trends in Customer Experience for 2024.
- McKinsey & Company. (2023). The Three Cs of Customer Satisfaction: Consistency, Consistency, Consistency.
- McKinsey & Company. (2022). How Customer Experience Drives Business Growth.
- PwC. (2023). Experience is Everything: Here's How to Get It Right.
- Qualtrics XM Institute. (2023). The ROI of Customer Experience.

- Salesforce. (2023). State of the Connected Customer – 6th Edition.

CX AND BUSINESS LITERATURE

- Bliss, J. (2015). Chief Customer Officer 2.0: How to Build Your Customer-Driven Growth Engine. Wiley.
- Dixon, M., Toman, N., & DeLisi, R. (2013). The Effortless Experience: Conquering the New Battleground for Customer Loyalty. Portfolio.
- Guidara, W. (2022). Unreasonable Hospitality: The Remarkable Power of Giving People More Than They Expect. Optimism Press.
- Heath, C., & Heath, D. (2017). The Power of Moments: Why Certain Experiences Have Extraordinary Impact. Simon & Schuster.
- Hurst, M., & Terry, P. (2014). Customers Included: How to Transform Products, Companies, and the World—With a Single Step. Creative Good Inc.

BRAND CASE STUDIES & EXAMPLES

- American Express—Empowered frontline experience culture.
- LEGO—Surprise-and-delight strategy and product input from service teams.
- REI—Customer-first return policies and ethical personalization stance.
- Southwest Airlines—Real-time CX insights and feedback via Qualtrics.
- Warby Parker—CX embedded in product design, policy, and feedback loops.
- Zappos—Long-call-time culture and employee empowerment around customer trust.

ABOUT THE AUTHOR

Lance Gruner is a globally recognized executive in customer experience, operations, and business transformation, with more than thirty years of leadership across Fortune 100 companies and fast-growing private enterprises. Throughout his career, Lance has led high-performing teams in over thirty countries and seventy-four languages, delivering world-class service, operational excellence, and measurable business results on a global scale.

Most recently, Lance served as executive vice president of Global Customer Care and Experience at Mastercard, where he oversaw one of the company's largest divisions and reported directly to the president and CTO. His leadership helped define and scale customer experience as a strategic differentiator, transforming how the company supported its partners, customers, and consumers worldwide.

His career also includes senior executive roles at Travelport, American Express, and Southfork Management Company, where he served as president and chief operating officer. Across these roles, Lance built and led global service and operations functions, drove digital transformation initiatives, and championed cultures rooted in accountability, empathy, and customer trust.

As a long-standing advisory board member for CMP's Customer Contact Week (CCW) and a respected industry voice, Lance has spent years advocating for the strategic value of customer experience at the highest levels. He continues to coach CX leaders, advise C-suite executives, and help organizations design systems that deliver both human impact and business value.

Lance's mission is clear: to educate, inspire, and elevate the customer experience profession—and to ensure the customer always has a seat at the decision-making table.

He lives in Nashville, Tennessee, where he remains active in mentoring, speaking, and consulting at the intersection of AI, experience design, and leadership.

Contact Information

For more information, visit www.LanceGruner.com.

Email: lance@lancegruner.com

Connect on LinkedIn: linkedin.com/in/LanceGruner